Woodbourne Library
Washington-Centerville Public Library
Centerville, Ohio

DISCARD

'I have learne _____ performance. Receiving er _____ my coach and team members have been absolutely vital to my success. This book will show you how.'
Amy Williams MBE, Olympic gold medallist

'Rob's new book *Blamestorming* provides highly practical tools to advance our psychological evolution through being cooperative rather than competitive in our communication with each other.'
Sir John Whitmore, author of the bestselling Coaching for Performance

'*Blamestorming* reveals how the way we think influences the way we communicate. This is cutting-edge psychology packaged in the most accessible way. Anyone who is serious about improving their communication skills will find it practical and relevant.'
Rob Archer, The Career Psychologist

'Rob's book will teach you how to hear what's really being said and say what you really mean to say. It will help you to increase your self-confidence and to put your relationships on a firmer and more positive footing. As texts, emails and other forms of "silent" communication crowd out the opportunity to practise the art of face-to-face conversation, we need the help of a skilled communicator more than ever. I recommend Rob's book to anyone who wants to communicate more effectively.'
Linda Blair, clinical psychologist, author, columnist, broadcaster

'Rob understands the dynamics of conversation inside out. He has vast experience and mastery in this field. The world will be better for him sharing it.'
Hugh Brasher, Race Director, London Marathon

'*Blamestorming* offers a truly fascinating insight into the complex world of conversation.'
Martin Davies, bestselling author of The Conjuror's Bird

'As the CEO of 55,000 staff, I have valued Rob's partnership at defining moments in our history. He knows how to have meaningful conversations that move life instead of talking about life. In *Blamestorming*, he will show you how.'
Julian Roberts, CEO, Old Mutual Group

D1404241

'In professional sport, as in every domain of life, conversation plays a crucial role in performance. In this book, Rob demonstrates simple, practical ways to revolutionize your conversational life.'
Matt Perry, England's most-capped rugby full-back

'Rob knows how to have meaningful conversations that allow people to be honest with themselves and authentic with others. I can't think of a better person to write a book like this!'
Paula Vennells, MD, Post Office Ltd (11,500 UK post offices)

'In *Blamestorming* Rob shares a wealth of experience and makes the art, science and skills of conversation accessible to everyone. Rob can be for conversation what Martin Lewis is for saving money – the UK's expert. Nobody occupies this space in the public consciousness today.'
Gordon Gourlay, MD, First Rate Exchange Services (the UK's leading provider of foreign exchange)

'As Headteacher with 440 pupils and 60 staff, my life is spent in conversation. *Blamestorming* will equip you with practical tools for communicating with others in a clear, sensitive and positive manner.'
Mark Stubbings, Headteacher, Brookfield Primary School (an inner London school where 25 per cent of students speak English as a second language)

BLAMESTORMING

Rob Kendall

BLAMESTORMING

Why conversations go wrong and how to fix them

W

WATKINS PUBLISHING

LONDON

This edition first published in the UK and USA 2014 by
Watkins Publishing Limited
PO Box 883, Oxford, OX1 9PL, UK

A member of Osprey Group

For enquiries in the USA and Canada:
Osprey Publishing, PO Box 3985, New York, NY 10185-3985
Tel: (001) 212 753 4402
Email: info@ospreypublishing.com

Design and typography copyright © Watkins Publishing Limited 2014
Text copyright © Rob Kendall 2014

Rob Kendall has asserted his right under the Copyright, Designs and Patents Act 1988
to be identified as the author of this work.

All rights reserved. No part of this book may be reproduced or utilized in any form
or by any means, electronic or mechanical,without prior permission in writing from
the Publishers.

10 9 8 7 6 5 4 3 2 1

Managing Editor: Sandra Rigby
Senior Editor: Fiona Robertson
Managing Designer: Suzanne Tuhrim
Illustrator: Richard Horne

Printed and bound in China

A CIP record for this book is available from the British Library

ISBN: 978-1-78028-654-9

Watkins Publishing is supporting the Woodland Trust, the UK's leading woodland
conservation charity, by funding tree-planting initiatives and woodland maintenance.

www.watkinspublishing.co.uk

CONTENTS

**CHAPTER
ONE**

BE CURIOUS
Why You Should Read *Blamestorming*; How It Works; and First Steps to Better Conversations

Our lives are conducted through conversations of one kind or another – in person and in groups, in formal and less formal situations, on the phone or by email – it's something we just do, most of the time without even thinking about it. We take our ability to converse for granted and when something goes wrong we tend to pick ourselves up and start over – usually without asking ourselves why or realizing that there are things we could have done to avoid the conversation going off track in the first place.

Generally, learning to talk to other people goes hand-in-hand with learning to speak. We learn through the example of others, by copying. It just happens, more or less. When we do communicate well the day-to-day things flow more smoothly and far more pleasantly. When we don't, the effects can be catastrophic. But, far from simply being something we started doing way back before we can remember – and accepting our relative skill, or lack of skill, as a given – conversation is something we can learn to do better and even excel in.

The fact is, conversations get tangled up all the time. What you'd thought would be a straightforward chat with your partner turns into a flaming row. Your teenage daughter reacts to a well-intended comment and storms out. A work meeting's fast feeling as if it's a waste of time because no one's listening. You prepare what you want to say in a tricky conversation and end up not saying what you'd meant to. You initiate a difficult conversation with a colleague and inadvertently put him or her on the defensive. A lot of the time you find yourself wondering what went wrong but you can't stop repeating the process again and again.

TRICKY SITUATIONS

Blamestorming focuses on four fundamental situations:

[1] **The Tangle** – where crossed wires lead to uncertainty and confusion, uncoordinated action and frustrated expectations.

How often do you shake your head in bewilderment and wonder how on earth a mix-up occurred? We'll explore how adapting your style of communication, setting the context and checking for clarity can help prevent misunderstanding and confusion.

[2] **The Big Argument** – where a convivial start has spiralled out of control and into a bitter row with a partner, a family member, a work colleague, a neighbour or anyone else you'd had no intention of falling out with.

Throughout the book we'll examine why conversations escalate into arguments, why the subtext of the argument can be more important than the content and how you can keep things at ground level.

[3] **The Bad Place** – where the conversation you were having with someone has gone horribly wrong and you're in the mire. Or where you simply feel disconnected and fed up with someone, and are left wondering how you're going to address the issue or recover the situation.

Getting into the Bad Place from time to time is part and parcel of any relationship, but you'd probably like to get into it far less often and, when you do, be there for less time. *Blamestorming* will show you how.

[4] **The Lock Down** – where feelings and thoughts are internalized or withheld and negative conclusions are drawn, leading to an implosion rather than to the explosion of the Big Argument.

If someone's in the Lock Down, they'll withdraw and won't want to talk, even though it's obvious they're deeply upset. This book offers ways to restore communication and bring your relationship back on an even keel.

Through a series of accessible and easy-to-follow techniques, *Blamestorming* will help you to avoid the pitfalls that sabotage conversations even when they've been started with the best of intentions. It shows you how your survival instincts often take over and derail your conversations at the worst possible moments. It reveals the warning signs that indicate when a conversation is beginning to go wrong before it's too late to turn back and, if it already has, this book shows you how to extricate yourself with the relationship intact.

Above all *Blamestorming* provides the insight and skills for consistently effective and rewarding interactions with others – and greater confidence that your conversations will go where and how you want them to.

WHAT DO I MEAN BY CONVERSATION?

Sandwiched somewhere between 'convent' and 'convoluted', a conversation is described by the *Oxford English Dictionary* as: 'A talk, especially an informal one, between two or more people, in which news and ideas are exchanged.'

What do we mean by talk?[1] Before the telephone came along, it meant two people communicating within shouting distance of each other, but Alexander Graham Bell changed all that. In the past 20 years the world has turned on its head again. We've now got more to consider. What about chatting online … and emailing … and texting? Are they talk? Where do we draw the line? I'd argue that conversation is no longer limited just to the *spoken* word. When I use online chat to keep in touch with my teenage children, I feel as though I'm *having a conversation* with them, and we happily exchange news and trivia together. That leaves texting and emailing. For the purposes of *Blamestorming*, I'm treating them as conversations too – so long as they're two-way.

Our interactions may be good or bad, inspiring or depressing. Occasionally, we may have an amazing dialogue at work, but more often than not conversations involve people talking over one another, trampling on each other's sentences or interjecting while the speaker is in mid-breath. Kitchen-table discussions can be sublimely enjoyable but can become tetchy all too easily, getting stuck in a depressingly familiar cycle. Conversations with our friends can be deeply fulfilling and enriching, but can also slide into misunderstanding and estrangement, leaving us confused about where it all went wrong. In this book I'll address how to have more conversations that are uplifting and fewer that are disheartening. The truth is, some conversations work out and others don't, but there's a lot you can do to ensure that more of yours do.

Most of us spend a staggering proportion of our waking life having conversations of one kind or another. For teachers, people in customer-facing roles or managers of teams, more than 75 per cent of the average day can involve interacting with others, whether face-to-face, via phone, email or online. Conversations are central to our lives. Yet, when I ask teenagers how much time they spend at school studying the skills necessary for successful conversation, I'm met with blank looks. It's an unacknowledged issue. People may be particularly adept in their subject areas, but the progress of so many talented and intelligent individuals is constrained because their skills in conversation have never advanced from being merely functional to being expert.

HOW THE BOOK WORKS

Each chapter in *Blamestorming* is short and self-contained, focusing on a specific topic with clear steps for action and a key lesson. I'd recommend reading the whole book and then returning to the chapters that you feel are most useful for you.

To make it easier for you to navigate your way through the different types of conversation, *Blamestorming* includes a cast of characters (each with his or her own icon, as shown below) in a variety of situations in which they experience conversations that go wrong. In each case, I explain how they could change the way they speak and listen in order to achieve a positive outcome.

Beth and Dan are both aged 27. Dan is assistant manager of a retail store and Beth is a teacher at the local primary school. She's applying for jobs as a deputy head, which involves a demanding interview process. Beth and Dan find that trivial conversations can quickly escalate into full-blown arguments.

Lara and Ethan: Lara (33) is married to Ethan (32) and is full-time mother to Jack (7) and Anna (5). Ethan is Dan's elder brother and a bit of a hotshot in the City, working for a bank based in London and New York. Ethan and Lara have different styles of communication, which often leads to misunderstandings and disagreements.

Ravi and Mia: Mia (36) is a social worker, married to Ravi (38), who's an IT manager. Their children are Yash (13), Ria (12) and Jay (10), all of whom present their own challenges when it comes to communication. Mia is an old friend of Lara's. They used to be inseparable but now see each other less often, which puts a strain on their friendship. Lara would like to talk with Mia about this, but fears for their relationship.

Diane (44) is headteacher of a primary school and Beth's boss. As a single parent, she juggles the pressures of her job with taking care of her children, Abby (17) and Ben (15). Diane treads the tightrope between not being a pushover for her teenagers and not constantly battling with them.

Bill lives next door to Beth and Dan; he is in his 50s. He's very opinionated. Dan tends to avoid him but, as he's not about to move house, needs to find ways to get on with him.

Lily is Dan and Ethan's mum. She's in her 60s and was widowed two years ago. She's quite lonely and loves seeing her sons, daughters-in-law and grandchildren, but she also likes her own space. Ethan tries to offer her advice but finds that she doesn't welcome it.

The characters display different personalities and styles of communication, as they balance the demands of work with the challenges involved in maintaining happy and healthy relationships at home. The conversations quoted in *Blamestorming* are largely adapted from accounts of real situations, as well as transcripts of actual conversations.

MY OWN JOURNEY

My understanding of the field of communication has been gleaned more through experience than academic study. As an introverted 18-year-old I had the humbling experience of working in India with amputees taking their first uncertain steps toward rebuilding their shattered lives. Speaking no Hindi, my method of communication with them involved sign language, drinking immense quantities of tea and – much to their amusement – drawing portraits of them in my sketchbook. This set the tone for an eclectic career, during which I've been a professional artist, consultant and entrepreneur. It's also included an underlying quest to understand the dynamics of effective communication. In the process I've been privileged to work with tens of thousands of people on every continent, ranging from leaders of large organizations to entrepreneurs, sports professionals, people living in conflict zones and teenage students.

As a father I've experienced the awe and terror of having a newborn child in my arms while wondering where the manual on parenting was. In the blink of an eye, I've watched our children grow into adults and had to learn to communicate with them in new ways. Learning how to be a loving husband and father has been the toughest challenge I've ever faced, and by far the most rewarding.

No great artist or writer would ever dream of saying that they've learned everything there is to know about their medium. Equally, I can make no claims to mastery of conversation, but I remain infinitely curious and keen to learn and improve. When it comes to conversation, we all muck things up and the ongoing challenge is ever present: can we get it right more often than we get it wrong and can we get better at conducting the conversations that really count? The answer is a resounding yes!

WHAT TO DO?

STEP 1:
Observe Conversations

Becoming an expert starts with being curious about the dynamics of conversation. Take time to consciously step back from the content of conversations you're having and observe what moves them forward or brings them to a grinding halt:

- Watch how a work meeting spirals out of control when there are no pauses between people speaking and how it becomes a contest for people to get their word in.
- When you give someone advice, listen for whether their response starts with 'Yes, but …' If it does, then maybe they aren't looking for your advice.
- Notice when an email exchange is in danger of getting out of control and sleep on it overnight before firing off an exasperated reply.
- Consider why someone says, 'All I'm saying is …' at the start of a sentence. Perhaps they don't feel that you listened to the last thing they said.
- Recognize how your conversational style changes when you're stressed or under pressure, and whether you get more directive or withdrawn. At these moments it's easy to conclude that other people are being awkward and rude, forgetting that our own interpretations and responses may be contributing to the problem.

Daily life offers you endless opportunities for noticing how a comment, pause or nod of acknowledgement can change the direction of a conversation – for better or worse. Rather than moving blindly through your interactions, keep an eye on what's happening while you're involved in conversation and keep an open, non-judgmental ear tuned in to the conversations people have around you.

Lesson 1: Don't just be in conversations, observe them.

CHAPTER
TWO

SPOT THE SIGNS
How to Tell When a Conversation Is Starting to Go Wrong

For 99 per cent of human existence, people lived as foragers in small, tight-knit communities where they were hardwired with certain survival instincts – to seek food, shelter, protection against aggressors and a sense of belonging. When plotted against this timeline, the development of the printing press, the telephone and the internet have all happened in the blink of an eye. Each of them has transformed the way we speak, listen and communicate. Yet, despite embedding these technologies in societies across the globe, the human brain remains more attuned to the world of our distant ancestors than to our brave new world.

What implications does this have for the way we conduct conversations? Under pressure, our survival instincts are liable to kick in, based on elementary desires for control, certainty and self-protection that surely stretch back into prehistory and often remain dominant in our interactions with others. The boy who knocks over a drink and instantly blames his sister is making an instinctive and defensive response, without any consideration or reflection. So is the mother who shouts at her child in frustration even though she knows it will spark the Big Argument, and the work colleagues who recognize the crucial role of listening and yet can't seem to keep quiet. The fact is that many of our behaviours are 'mindless' – the flip side of mindful – in the sense that they are knee-jerk or 'shotgun' responses which, on subsequent reflection, are unhelpful, ill-conceived or even untrue.[1] In these situations, we know we should think before we speak, or find our voice instead of remaining mute, or make a phone call rather than firing off an intemperate email. But, for some reason, we don't.

Ellen Langer, Professor of Psychology at Harvard University and a world-leading expert on mindfulness, tells an anecdote that involved using her new credit card in a store. The cashier noticed that Langer's card wasn't signed and asked her to sign it. Once the sale had gone through and the receipt had been issued, the cashier asked Langer to sign that too. Holding the newly signed card in one hand, and the receipt in the other, the cashier compared the two signatures even though they'd both been written in front of her eyes.[2]

It takes a few moments for the flaw in the cashier's strategy to sink it. Her mistake is so easily made and yet makes no logical sense. Part of the problem is that conversations happen so fast, with barely a gap, or none at all, between one person finishing a sentence and another person starting theirs. In an effort to react quickly and conserve energy, the brain is inclined to accept the most readily available response to a situation, even if it subsequently appears to be a mindless one. For example, it takes far less cognitive effort for us to keep peddling a pre-existing view than to drop our righteousness and take on someone else's perspective. The result is that we tend to get caught up in patterns of conversational behaviour in which history repeats itself and our messy interactions can seem uncomfortably familiar.

THE WARNING LIGHTS

Take this example when Beth and Dan – who are both 27 and have been together for four years – find that their TV programme schedules clash after a demanding day at work:

Beth enters the front room, where Dan is sitting, engrossed in the TV:

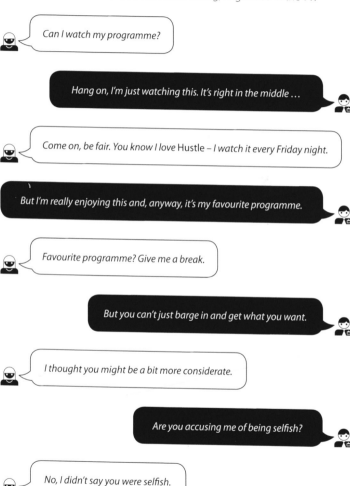

Can I watch my programme?

Hang on, I'm just watching this. It's right in the middle …

Come on, be fair. You know I love Hustle – I watch it every Friday night.

But I'm really enjoying this and, anyway, it's my favourite programme.

Favourite programme? Give me a break.

But you can't just barge in and get what you want.

I thought you might be a bit more considerate.

Are you accusing me of being selfish?

No, I didn't say you were selfish.

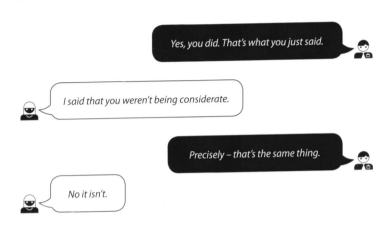

While, in terms of its usefulness, Dan and Beth's conversation is going absolutely nowhere, it's actually heading at high speed into the Big Argument and the Bad Place. On board planes, displays of warning lights alert pilots to impending danger and protect against unseen hazards and imminent disaster. Similarly, there are warning lights that appear in our conversations. We often either don't recognize them or choose to ignore them.

What are the signals that indicate Dan and Beth's conversation is heading into jeopardy? There are five signs to watch out for – think of them as warning lights that tell you when a conversation is going wrong.

[1] Blamestorming – when the accusations and criticisms are starting to fly and you notice you're beginning to sound alarmingly self-righteous.

If a conversation's starting to turn into a blame game, with someone being accused of being at fault, it's a clear signal of Blamestorming. You won't be interested in sharing responsibility, taking a balanced view or finding a pragmatic solution. You'll use language like 'they always' and 'you never', and you'll probably try to make yourself look like the innocent victim by loading the blame for an issue or problem on someone else's shoulders.

If the person you're blaming isn't the person you're having the conversation with, that person becomes an easy target because they can't defend themselves. In these kinds of situations people often build on each other's comments:

'He's useless'

'Yeah, worse than useless'

'Yeah, useless squared'

… and so on.

You're closing ranks, looking for people to concur with your point of view. It's like a snowball rolling downhill, increasing in size as it goes.

Having a Blamestorming conversation with someone who's in front of you is more like a boxing match. You'll start trading opinions with each other, in which the gist of the conversation is that it's the other person's fault. You may find yourself saying, 'I'm not arguing with you, I'm just explaining why you're wrong.'

How can you tell when you're Blamestorming? You'll find yourself being more committed to apportioning blame than to resolving issues.

[2] Escalation – when the temperature is starting to rise and your conversation seems to have become all about 'winning', regardless of the cost.

Escalation is what happens when your anger takes over. When you notice this warning signal you're either already in, or about to enter, the

Big Argument. You'll find yourself making wild and exaggerated claims, dragging up the past, drawing below-the-belt comparisons and making threats you're likely to regret later. When you're in Escalation you may find yourself saying at the top of your voice, 'Stop shouting!', to which the other person may bellow, 'I'm not shouting!'

The stakes can get pretty high when a conversation shifts into Escalation. If you fail to notice the signals you could end up cashing in all your chips as you try to win. Getting caught up in Escalation makes it difficult to see the full cost until it's become destructive and you've suddenly found yourself in the Bad Place.

How can you tell when you're Escalating? You'll notice the intensity of an argument increasing FAST.

[3] Yes, But … – when you dismiss someone's solutions because *you* want to be heard, or brush aside their opinions because they don't match yours. In truth, you're not really interested in their pearls of wisdom on the matter.

There's often a mismatch between what you're offering in a conversation and what someone else wants or needs. You might think you have the perfect solution to an issue or think you know what the other person ought to do, but they may have different ideas. Yes, But … is a contradiction in terms. When we say it, we usually mean 'No, and here's why'.

How can you tell when you're in Yes, But …? The short answer is that you'll notice yourself saying it.

[4] Dominatricks – when a conversation's flow and rhythm starts to fall apart because you're trying to take control and dominate.

You'll have spotted the signs of Dominatricks if you've noticed that you're finishing each other's sentences: that one or other of you is trying to drive the conversation on their terms, not listening to what's being said and not allowing space for the other's opinion or disagreement.

How can you tell when you're in Dominatricks? It feels competitive -- you'll notice you're interrupting the person you're speaking with and not taking time to pause, listen and reflect.

[5] Mixed Messages – when you're making assumptions and drawing conclusions that are out of step with reality, or when you're speaking at cross-purposes.

Like trains that pass in opposite directions, some conversations can feel as though you're on a different track going in the opposite direction to the other person. It might be that:

- The context isn't clear
- You're not addressing the sub-text of the conversation
- You're swapping preconceived ideas or opinions rather than listening
- You're replying to what you thought they said rather than what they *actually* said.

If you notice the warning light for Mixed Messages you may need to wind the conversation back to check that you're both clear about what's being discussed and that you understand each other, or to ascertain what you're both really trying to say.

How can you tell when you're in Mixed Messages? You feel puzzled or surprised about how a conversation seems to be unfolding or the conversation you're having feels as if it's somehow out of sync.

SEEING THE SIGNALS

How do the warning lights play out in Dan and Beth's conversation?

When Dan objects to Beth interrupting his programme, his words blurt out and he doesn't say what he means. If he'd stopped and thought about it, he might have said, 'I don't like it when you come in and tell me to change the TV channel.' Instead he ends up in a ridiculous situation in which he defends the idea that he's watching his favourite programme (even though he isn't) because he doesn't want to back down. It all happens in a split second. Suddenly, the warning lights are flashing and we can see:

- Dominatricks ('Hang on, I'm just watching this.')
- Blamestorming ('Yes, you did. That's what you just said.')
- Escalation ('Are you accusing me of being selfish?')
- Yes, But … ('But you can't just barge in …').

If Dan and Beth could see the warning lights flashing, they *could* change direction before the conversation leads them into the Bad Place.

WHAT TO DO?

STEP 1:
Notice the Warning Lights

In any area of life, warning lights are worthless if you don't notice them. That's why cars don't have grey indicator lights and why smoke alarms are so startling. They're designed to impose themselves on your consciousness. In the same way, you need to attend to the warning lights in your conversational life the moment they appear – not as an after-thought.

When you look out for them, you'll begin to notice the signs in all sorts of conversations, from your work meetings to your kitchen-table discussions. See if you can spot them in the conversations going on around you the next time you're on a train or in a restaurant.

Being able to spot the warning lights isn't a licence for you to point out what other people are doing wrong. For instance, if you accuse someone of Blamestorming, you're likely to be doing the very same thing yourself and pushing the conversation into Escalation. The warning signals act like an alert system, enabling you to make choices about how to best proceed.

STEP 2:
Consider Your Choices

The difficulty with choice is that it introduces the notion of responsibility. The easy option for Dan is to believe that Beth is being difficult and inconsiderate by barging in on him while he's watching the TV. Let's freeze their argument after Beth says:

> *Come on, be fair. You know I love* Hustle – *I watch it every Friday night.*

At this point, Dan has choices that might include:

Choice 1: He can claim that he's watching his favourite programme – this is his instinctive response.

Choice 2: He can seek to negotiate a reasonable solution – he might offer to record the rest of his programme or to record hers so that both of them can watch it afterwards.

Choice 3: He can say, 'No problem at all, I'll switch over when your programme starts.'

Choice 1 is survival based and requires little cognitive effort on Dan's part. Choices 2 and 3 are not so ready to hand. They require Dan to consider Beth's needs as well as his own.

Dan opts for Choice 1 and claims that he's watching his favourite programme. He doesn't even consider that there might be other choices he could have made. However, as soon as his words spill out, he recognizes that his statement rings untrue and it's obvious Beth knows it, too. After all, it's a natural history programme he's never seen before, albeit an interesting one. Beth immediately calls his bluff, saying:

Favourite programme? Give me a break.

At this point Dan faces another set of choices. Let's imagine these:

Choice 1: He can say, 'But you can't just barge in and get what you want.'
Choice 2: He can laugh at himself and say, 'Yeah, sorry. That was a completely bizarre thing for me to say.'
Choice 3: He can reconsider and say, 'OK, it's probably not my favourite, but I was enjoying it. Let's see if we can sort out a solution.'

If Dan follows his survival instincts he'll stick with Choice 1 because it comes to him easily and doesn't involve him having to think or backtrack. The irony of the situation is that he doesn't care that much about the programme he's watching when Beth comes in, but for some reason he digs his heels in.

The Dominatricks warning light is flashing, but Dan doesn't notice it. He and Beth are already in the Bad Place by the time he gets more perspective.

As you engage in conversation, start to acknowledge that you have choices about how you can respond at each stage. Once you do this, the next step is to develop your skill in making the best choice in the circumstances. The same principle applies with any discipline. With the ball at their feet, world-class footballers will see a series of choices that are invisible to the rest of us. At this level of the game, footballers have both the eyes to spot the options and the skills to exploit them more consistently.

Blamestorming will enable you to recognize the choices open to you when you're in the heat of a difficult conversation and give you the skills to turn things around to everyone's advantage.

Lesson 2: You always have a choice about how to respond.

CHAPTER
THREE

HOLD THE TRUTH LIGHTLY
Why We Think Negatively and How to Avoid Dramatizing Situations

We can all be prone to a bit of hyperbole. You may say, 'I'm starving', if you're an hour late for lunch, or, 'I won't fit into my jeans', if you're eyeing up a piece of cake and worrying about the consequences. We often exaggerate, and use comparisons and analogies to make a point. When Lady Gaga said, 'I live halfway between reality and theatre at all times', she was speaking for all of us. We don't have a choice about the circumstances we're born into but each of us has a say in the way we interpret life and how we describe it.

Without exaggeration life would be dull and Hollywood would be bankrupt. As the great producer Samuel Goldwyn once said, 'We want a story that starts out with an earthquake and works its way up to a climax.' [1] During our conversations it can be very tempting to intersperse the sharp facts of reality with the half-truths of dramatic interpretation. The problem with this is that it can all too often lead us into the Tangle and the Bad Place.

CREATING STORIES

Take this example: the bank that Dan's high-flying brother Ethan works for is merging with another organization. The facts of the situation are:

- The new organizational structure hasn't been finalized.
- Ethan's spoken to two other people who are worried about their future.
- Depending on their position, some people will need to reapply for their jobs.

- A month ago Ethan's CEO told him, 'I think you'll be fine,' but they haven't spoken since.
- While Ethan was at work yesterday, the leadership team spent six hours in meetings.

But this is how Ethan describes it to Dan, over a couple of beers:

> *We're all in a total vacuum and everyone's thinking the worst. It even looks like we're going to have to reapply for our jobs. It's unbelievable! My CEO said he thought I'd be safe, but that was months ago and he's blanked me ever since. It looks like I'm definitely heading for the exit. What nobody realizes is that I'm keeping the business afloat while they swan about, going from one meeting to the next.*

What Ethan's doing is taking the facts that he's aware of and creating his own story around them. While the facts are essentially neutral, Ethan's version of the situation casts his CEO as the villain while he plays the oppressed hero. By doing this, he encourages Dan to adopt his point of view and become an ally in his struggle against an adversary he's imagined.

There's nothing unique about what Ethan's doing. We all tend to follow this pattern. When we speak, we create an angle that plays to our advantage – it makes us look more heroic or more like the innocent victim. Our dramatization of events takes on more and more veracity each time we tell it, becoming increasingly concrete in our minds to the point where we think our characterization is a statement of truth.

GETTING STUCK IN A VIEW

So what's wrong with using a little artistic licence when it comes to interpreting events? Ethan isn't being intentionally deceptive or saying anything he doesn't actually believe, but there are two repercussions that he cannot clearly see:

[1] Ethan's version of events has a significant and negative influence on his own feelings. Read both the facts and Ethan's account of the situation again. While reading them, think about the *emotions* each might provoke. I'd argue that the facts don't incite a strong reaction, positive or negative. On the other hand, Ethan's story stirs up strong negative emotions. He feels:

- **Angry** ('It even looks like we're going to have to reapply for our jobs. It's unbelievable!')
- **Let down** ('My CEO said he thought I'd be safe, but that was months ago and he's blanked me ever since.')
- **Anxious** ('It looks like I'm definitely heading for the exit.')
- **Undervalued** ('What nobody realizes is that I'm keeping the business afloat while they swan about, going from one meeting to the next.').

The knock-on effect of Ethan's feelings is that they affect his productivity and morale at work and spill over into his home life. Jack and Anna, his young children, are noticing that he seems particularly grumpy – commenting to each other that, 'Dad seems very cross at the moment.' And his wife, Lara, is avoiding the topic of their summer holiday; she can see he's not in the right mood to listen or to think constructively.

[2] Ethan's interpretation of the situation *isn't true*! He's not in possession of all the facts. His view of the situation is merely an interpretation; one of many possible ways of looking at things. These are the pieces of information he's not privy to:

- Some people *will* need to reapply for their jobs – where there are overlaps – but this won't apply to Ethan's area.
- The directors have agreed that Ethan will run a newly merged team.
- The leadership team has decided not to communicate the details until the whole structure is agreed.

Against the background of these additional facts, Ethan's story falls apart. He's got into the Tangle and now the Bad Place, but it's all in his head and self-created. He's compounding the problem through the way he speaks about it. He really doesn't have to be in this situation. Of course, we're rarely in possession of all the facts, and it's understandable that someone would be anxious when there's a degree of uncertainty about the future. However, if Ethan could just hold the truth lightly, it would help him remain open to other interpretations of what's happening. Instead, he's reacted to his fear and anxiety, becoming narrow-minded and – to a degree – out of kilter with reality.

NEGATIVE BIAS AND FIXED POSITIONS

Our thinking tends to be negatively biased and we often focus on what's wrong rather than what's right. It's actually a highly effective survival mechanism that we carry with us from the distant past. Living the forager lifestyle, our ancestors were constantly on the lookout for aggressors – both human and animal. If you were peering into the gloom at dusk and saw a dark shape coming out of the bush toward you, would you assume that it's friend or foe? It would be sensible to err on the side of caution and be ready with the nearest means of defence, should it be the latter. As a child, before I went to sleep, I always used to make sure there weren't any monsters lurking under my bed. Even though I knew it was pretty unlikely, I still said to myself, 'Tonight might be the night!'

We used to need our survival instincts to make sure we lived to see another day and didn't wind up as the evening meal of a wild carnivore. There was, and sometimes still is, considerable value in acting as though the aggressor is there – until proven otherwise. If you have any doubt about whether or not your own survival instincts are intact, think about your reaction when you were last woken up in the night by a loud and unexpected noise. Alarm bells would have rung in your amygdalae, which form part of the limbic system, the part of your brain that governs emotions and behaviour, among other things. Instantaneous changes would have taken place: your heartbeat and blood pressure would have increased and hormones would have been released into your bloodstream in preparation for a fight-or-flight response. In less than a second you would have shifted from being in a deep sleep to sitting bolt upright, while the information available to you reached your cortex and you were able to formulate a rational explanation. If all was well, you may have sunk back into sleep while in the background your survival instincts remained on guard.

At times, we all adopt a defensive stance in case things don't go to plan. Ethan is mentally and emotionally preparing himself for the possibility that he'll lose his job, by adopting a negative and fixed attitude. This is reflected in his Blamestorming conversations. But there's a price to be paid. His stress levels are running high and his emotional state is having an impact on Lara and the children. If he could hold the truth lightly and be more flexible in his thinking, he would experience less stress.

WHAT TO DO?

STEP 1:
Manage Your Mind

When Ethan speaks to Dan, it would be more useful if he separated the facts of the situation from the stories going on in his head. Rather than saying, 'We're all in a total vacuum and everyone's thinking the worst …', he could have said, 'I've spoken to a couple of other people who are worried about their jobs.' And instead of saying, 'It looks like I'm definitely heading for the exit,' he could have emphasized the fact that his CEO had told him, 'I think you'll be safe,' without adding the comment about being blanked. Bear in mind, though, that this mental sorting process isn't instinctive and it does take discipline.

If Ethan managed to do this, he could avoid talking himself into a drama. He'd realize that his interpretation of the situation at work amounts to a lengthy collection of stories based on a sparse list of facts. He'd understand that there are a number of ways to interpret the facts and that he doesn't have to get stuck in any one of them. If he feels that facts are rather thin on the ground, there's probably someone he can go to for more information.

STEP 2:
Own Your Own Story

Imagine two people sitting opposite each other, pointing their fingers and saying, 'You always do this,' and, 'You never do that.' Now imagine these same two people saying, 'My story about you is that you always do this and you never do that.' The difference is that the second version balances the responsibility between the person who is supposedly at fault and the author of the story – and, technically, it's accurate. Taking this approach helps avoid falling into Dominatricks or Blamestorming.

If Ethan had done this he'd easily have been able to adjust the way he talked about his work situation. If he prefaced his account of the situation by saying to Dan, 'This is my story about what's happening', it would have signalled to both of them that it's just that – a story.

I worked with an organizational team whose members would say, 'You seem to be in a different story to me,' when they reached an apparent disagreement with each other. It was a reminder to loosen the grip on their own version of the truth and an invitation to explore each other's version more deeply.

Lesson 3: Explore different versions of the truth, taking responsibility for your own.

CHAPTER FOUR

STAND CLEAR OF THE ESCALATORS
How to Prevent Trivial Conversations Becoming Toxic Arguments

The explorer Deborah Shapiro spent 15 months on the Antarctic Peninsula with her husband Rolf. Nine of these months were in complete isolation. When they returned to civilization, people wanted to know how they'd managed to avoid killing each other. They replied that, since they relied on each other for survival, murder would have been counterproductive.[1] But they did cite the example of a man killing his colleague over a chess game when stationed at a remote Antarctic station. As Shapiro pointed out, the tragedy could have started from him not liking the way his colleague buttered his toast – and ended up in homicide.

Research shows that most arguments start as a result of trivial irritations such as leaving dirty clothes on the floor, not doing the washing-up and flicking TV channels. Switching the channel while your partner's out of the room is guaranteed to spark a row and, if you try removing the batteries from the remote control so the channel can't be changed while you visit the bathroom, you may be risking a nuclear reaction.

Starting out seemingly simple, these situations can quickly spiral to a point where the people involved are questioning their relationships.

THE SPIRAL

One Tuesday, Beth gets home first after work and begins preparing a meal for herself and Dan. She gets a text from Dan saying:

```
Sorry. delayed @ work. on my way. c u soon xx
```

When Dan eventually gets home, this is their conversation:

You've been ages. Your food's cold.

Sorry … I had to stop for a lightning pint with Ethan.
He needed some moral support.

Oh, so you weren't working late.

I was, but Ethan's having a work crisis and he
collared me for a 10-minute pint.

10 minutes??!!

OK, it was a bit longer, but don't get this out
of perspective.

Perspective! Your text said you were at work. I'd call that a lie!

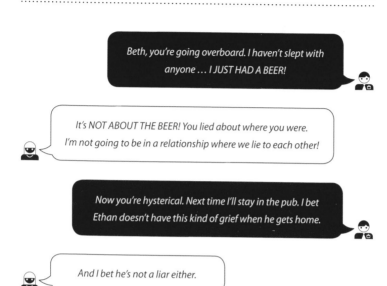

Beth, you're going overboard. I haven't slept with anyone ... I JUST HAD A BEER!

It's NOT ABOUT THE BEER! You lied about where you were. I'm not going to be in a relationship where we lie to each other!

Now you're hysterical. Next time I'll stay in the pub. I bet Ethan doesn't have this kind of grief when he gets home.

And I bet he's not a liar either.

(She leaves the room, slamming the door.)

In less than a minute, Dan and Beth are in the Bad Place. Each comment has taken the intensity and volume of their argument to another level, and the lid has been blown off any chance of their having a constructive conversation. Afterwards they feel angry, misunderstood, bewildered and – for a while at least – right about their point of view.

WHAT WAS THAT ABOUT?

Comparing what happened to the launch of an Apollo rocket can help us get to the bottom of Dan and Beth's exchange. Just like them, the rocket that put the first man on the moon reached maximum velocity in a number of stages. Burning vast quantities of kerosene and liquid oxygen, the engines generated incredible thrust, firing the rocket 42 miles into the sky in less than 3 minutes. At this point its first stage dropped away and its second-stage engines fired up, using liquid hydrogen and oxygen as fuel to push it into space. Hurtling out of the Earth's atmosphere, the rocket discarded its second stage, while its third-stage engines took over – propelling it on its course to the moon.

Beth and Dan have gone through their own mini lift-off – this also happened in stages:

First Stage: creating the spark for an argument – Dan was telling the truth when he said he was working late. What he didn't do was let Beth know he'd got a last-minute call from Ethan inviting him for a quick pint. If he'd told her that Ethan seemed a bit troubled and they were going for a drink, she probably would have understood and wouldn't have made the effort of cooking for him. It's often the small things, which could be avoided, that ignite an argument.

Second Stage: accusations and justifications – Having stewed for an hour waiting for Dan to come home, Beth is upset and gets on the front foot as soon as the door opens. Accusations and justifications create the thrust that blast Beth and Dan into a confrontation. The more she accuses, the more he defends his position, claiming that he made a generous sacrifice for his brother and inferring that she's over-reacting. Her feelings of anger intensify; the more accusing she becomes, the more hard-done-by he feels.

There is another way Dan could have reacted, meeting Beth's accusations with counter-accusations rather than a justification. It would go like this:

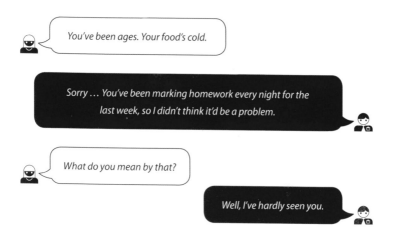

You've been ages. Your food's cold.

Sorry ... You've been marking homework every night for the last week, so I didn't think it'd be a problem.

What do you mean by that?

Well, I've hardly seen you.

Dan would be taking the front-foot position, diverting the conversation from his going to the pub and catching Beth off-guard. The result would be much the same. Accusations and justifications, or accusations and counter-accusations, are strategies we employ to win a disagreement but they also act as the fuel that allow an argument to take off, pushing it into orbit.

Escalation isn't the only warning light that's flashing; Dominatricks is, too. And Dominatricks is not conducive to listening. Neither Beth nor Dan is willing to back down or cede control, and there are no pauses in the conversation, so it becomes a battle of righteousness. Feeling they're not being heard intensifies their anger, which adds more fuel to their face-off.

Third Stage: comparisons and threats – As an argument gets further and further off the ground it reaches a point where courtesy, consideration and good manners are totally abandoned and people simply let rip. Beth and Dan reach this point when they move into comparisons and threats.

First, in an attempt to make Beth feel as if she's being over the top, Dan downplays his misdemeanour by comparing it to sleeping with someone. Seeing through his tactic, and riled by it, Beth opts for a threat. When she says, 'I'm not going to be in a relationship where we lie to each other!' she clearly means, 'I don't want to be in a relationship where you lie to me!' Stung by this, Dan makes a comparison with Lara, which he knows will get through Beth's defences. Beth's parting shot and the slammed door announce that the argument has reached its climax, and they find separate places to seethe and eventually cool down.

It's important to remember that arguments are a healthy part of any relationship, but when they get out of control they can become destructive, at least if they're not cleared up effectively. Beth and Dan never meant their argument to get so vitriolic. At times the process of Escalation accelerates at breakneck speed and without any mindful consideration of what's happening and where it's going. It's a verbal scrap in which all sorts of tricks come into play, with threat being your ace. You get so focused on winning the argument, you don't notice the damage and hurt you may be causing – till it's too late.

WHAT TO DO?

STEP 1:
Keep Your Conversations at Ground Level
Here are three things Dan could have done to avoid him and Beth ending up in the Bad Place. Try them if you find yourself in a similar situation.

[1] He could have **listened to Beth without interrupting**, even if she had a lot to say. When you disagree with someone, the tendency is to interject. It's counter-intuitive not to, but with practice becomes easier. It would have slowed down the pace and intensity of their conversation and made Beth feel that she was being listened to.

> *I'm exhausted; I had a full-on day … I went shopping on the way home, then cooked a meal … and I had absolutely no idea that you were off for a pint with Ethan … you didn't even bother to call!*

[2] He could have **acknowledged Beth's feelings and empathized with her**. If he'd done that sincerely, with absolutely no sarcasm in his voice, it could have had a remarkable effect on the situation. When a conversation escalates, both parties start feeling anger in one form or another – irritation, annoyance or frustration. If feelings aren't being heard or acknowledged, they increase in intensity. If he'd acknowledged her feelings, Beth wouldn't have needed to escalate them.

> *You cooked for us both … then had to eat alone while my dinner went cold … plus you couldn't reach me … it's wrecked your evening.*

[3] He could have **called to let Beth know what he was doing** before going to the pub. If he'd done this, he could have reframed her expectations and avoided subsequent problems. Even if he hadn't, once he'd come home he could have got the conversation back to ground level by thanking Beth for preparing a meal, and apologizing for being inconsiderate and not calling. There's every chance she would have accepted this, so long as he made no attempt to prove his innocence or shift the blame on to her.

> *I'm really sorry, Beth. I just didn't think. I should have called you after Ethan called me, before I left the office. Thanks for cooking for me.*

STEP 2:
Press STOP!

Putting a conversation on hold is easier than you might think. Without making it an Oscar-winning exit, create some distance from the conversation by removing yourself physically from it – even for a minute or two. Tell the other person you need to go to the bathroom, get some air or water. It'll give you some crucial thinking time and help you regain your centre.

If you're in a work meeting, make whatever excuse seems appropriate to leave the room for a few minutes. If you're at home you may have to be a bit more insistent about needing your own space because the person you're talking to may not want to stop. Beth could have tackled it this way in her conversation with Dan:

I need to take some time out from this conversation before it gets worse.

Hang on a minute. You can't back out now.

Sorry, I'm feeling really upset. I need to stop this and come back to it later.

It may feel a bit uncomfortable but it's a useful thing to be able to do. It immediately defuses a confrontation and helps stop it becoming destructive.

STEP 3:
Listen to What You're Saying

Keep your attention on what you're saying to spot the warning signs as soon as they appear. Exaggerations, accusations, comparisons and threats all point to Escalation. If you notice that they're being used in a conversation, it's time to bring it back down. Being aware of what's happening in a conversation gives you the chance to steer another course. Noticing the signals is your key to being able to do this.

Lesson 4: Practise bringing your conversations back to ground level and keeping them there.

CHAPTER
FIVE

IDENTIFY THE SUBTEXT
How to Decipher What People Really Mean When They Speak

Some conversations can be bewildering. You could be sitting three feet away from someone and feel as though you're worlds apart. The Tangle isn't only the result of people not listening to each other. It also happens when what you say is not what you really mean. Like in a good novel, in a conversation the real action may be happening in the sub-plot – hidden from view.

I once had a row with my wife, Sally, when a family friend was staying. We started quarrelling about what soup to cook for lunch, then about how much everyone would want. After a couple of minutes our friend cut across our arguing, 'You do realize this argument isn't about the soup, don't you?'

Her comment stopped us in our tracks. She was right. Our minor irritations with each other had spilled into this conversation about lunch. It's a fact; most arguments are *not about the issue you're talking about*. It can make it very difficult to resolve disagreements – you're actually having the wrong conversation. Sally and I were never going to sort out our frustrations with each other while we stayed on the subject of soup.

Most arguments aren't about the issue you think you're fighting about. The real issues lie below the surface, either unseen or unacknowledged. One of the secrets of being a consummate conversationalist is the ability to get better at identifying and addressing the subtext of a conversation before it starts heading toward the Tangle, the Big Argument or the Bad Place.

It's important to make a distinction between the content of a conversation – the words that are actually being spoken – and the subtext. Often, what's happening beneath the surface is actually running the show.

AIR FLORIDA FLIGHT 90

Failing to understand subtext can have disastrous consequences. Look at the following extracts, taken from the black box recording of the captain on Air Florida Flight 90 and his first officer who had concerns prior to taking off and crashing in icy conditions on 13 January 1982 – a disaster that led to the deaths of 78 people.[1] The lightly shaded boxes show what the subtext might have been:

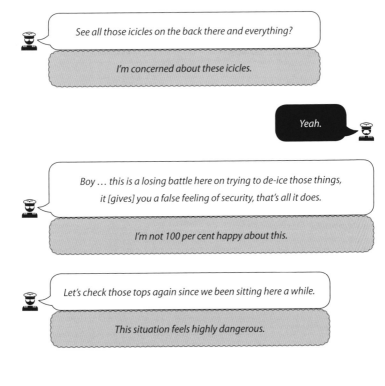

> *See all those icicles on the back there and everything?*

> *I'm concerned about these icicles.*

> *Yeah.*

> *Boy ... this is a losing battle here on trying to de-ice those things, it [gives] you a false feeling of security, that's all it does.*

> *I'm not 100 per cent happy about this.*

> *Let's check those tops again since we been sitting here a while.*

> *This situation feels highly dangerous.*

(In reference to instrument readings)

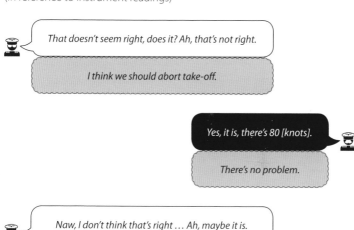

> *That doesn't seem right, does it? Ah, that's not right.*

> *I think we should abort take-off.*

> *Yes, it is, there's 80 [knots].*

> *There's no problem.*

> *Naw, I don't think that's right … Ah, maybe it is.*

The first officer leaves multiple clues that he's concerned about the inclement weather but the captain doesn't pick up on them. His attention is focused on getting the flight underway.

Why didn't the first officer say, 'Stop the flight!'?

The conclusion of the post-crash investigation was that he held back because of an unconscious belief that *first officers don't tell captains what to do.* As a result, he implied his concerns without making them explicit.

And why didn't the captain ask his first officer, 'Are you worried about taking off?'

Both of them skirted around the conversation that needed to happen to avoid the disaster. The crash investigation prompted an overhaul of pilots' training across the aviation industry, insisting that first officers be more assertive when raising concerns and that captains respond more decisively.

HOW DO YOU CRACK THE CODE?

There's a story of an African tribal chief whose communication skills were legendary across the land. A young man from a neighbouring district went to one of his tribal meetings, determined to learn from his skills. He noticed that each time a villager asked a question the chief answered it in a way that the young man hadn't at all anticipated. Each time the questioner sat down seemingly satisfied with the chief's answer.

The young man waited until the meeting was over before approaching the chief. 'Your Highness, what is the secret behind your answers to these people's questions?' he asked.

'I don't answer the question,' the chief replied. 'I answer what gave rise to the question.'

We tend to get caught up in the content of a conversation because it's easier to address. Responding to what people say can be hard enough without trying to listen to what they're not saying. But whether a conversation is happening in the kitchen, the bedroom, the boardroom or the cockpit of a plane, we'd benefit from increasing our ability to decode the subtext.

During the Second World War the British government recruited a team of mathematical wizards as code-breakers. They developed the Colossus, a huge computer-like machine that filled an entire room, and used it to decipher encoded messages being sent from the German Lorenz machine. The Colossus was capable of reading intercepted messages at the rate of 5,000 characters per second.[2] You may think you need your own Colossus machine to work out what's happening in the subtext of a conversation.

Fortunately, you don't, even though getting beneath the surface of what's being said is not always easy.

Lara (Ethan's wife) has an old friend from university called Mia whose style of communication is very different to that of her husband, Ravi. He's more reflective than Mia, tending to keep his thoughts and concerns to himself until he's mentally processed them. This has a knock-on effect for her because, although she can tell he's unhappy about something, she doesn't necessarily know what's troubling him. There are times when she feels she's not getting anywhere.

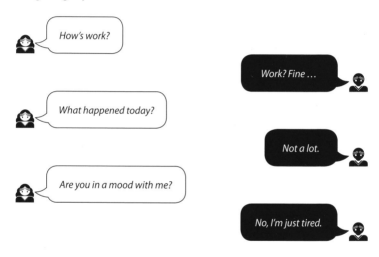

How's work?

Work? Fine ...

What happened today?

Not a lot.

Are you in a mood with me?

No, I'm just tired.

Ravi's monosyllabic responses could either encourage Mia to change the subject or wind her up to the point where she starts feeling frustrated and accuses Ravi of being distant and uncommunicative, which will make him withdraw even further. It's easy to see how a conversation like this could go from the Tangle to the Big Argument and finally end up in the Bad Place.

Being able to decode the subtext can stop that from happening.

WHAT TO DO?

STEP 1:
Ask Questions to Identify the Subtext and Listen

Mia assumes Ravi's in a mood with her. If she asks questions that encourage Ravi to give a deeper response, she's likely to make more progress.

> *I've noticed you've stopped talking about work recently and you seem really flat when you come home. What's happening?*

> *It's a bit rubbish, but nothing I can't deal with.*

> *What's rubbish?*

> *Well, Steve [Ravi's boss] is being a bit of a pain.*

> *Oh, OK, so what's happening with Steve? What's he doing?*

> *He seems to be sidelining me. He used to ask for my advice all the time, but now he's always in meetings with Chris. I don't know why things have changed and I don't know what they're planning.*

When did you first notice that?

Well, it was fine until the start of the project we're working on at the moment, and then …

Decoding the subtext of a conversation is a process. It usually takes more than just one question. Rather than stopping after her first question, Mia goes on asking questions that reflect what Ravi's just said – while listening and being totally supportive. Each question she asks invites Ravi to go a bit further and explain himself, rather than just giving a 'yes' or 'no' answer.

If you follow through like this you can usually get below the surface to the real issue, without making the other person back off. You'll probably find they appreciate the chance to talk in more detail, feeling they're being heard and having an opportunity to move things forward by talking them through.

Throughout their conversation Mia avoids making judgments or offering her opinion. If she'd done this, it would have broken the thread and interrupted Ravi's flow.

The questions you ask, and the way in which you ask them, will vary depending on the context, but the principle is basically the same: ask questions that invite a deeper response, following through with a line of questions that reflect what you're being told in the answers you're getting.

If you ask a monosyllabic teenager, 'How's school?', you're likely to end up with a one-word answer. But if you use this as an opener and then follow through with questions that encourage them to share their thoughts and feelings, you'll open the door for them to express themselves more deeply.

You can use the same principle of inquiry when trying to decode the subtext of any conversation.

STEP 2:
Communicate Your Own Subtext

Lara is fighting a losing battle to get Jack and Anna, her children, to keep their rooms tidy. She's fed up with feeling as if she's their maid and her usual response tends to be along the lines of:

> *You never pick your clothes up off the floor! Both of you – you're bone idle!*

Lara's not saying what she really feels and, rather than achieving anything constructive, her response is more likely to put her children on the defensive because it's accusatory. It's also unlikely that she'd be able to justify her use of the word 'never' if Jack or Anna challenged her on it.

Lara needs to **identify her subtext and bring it to the foreground** of any conversation she has about the issue. It would also be better if she spoke to Jack and Anna separately.

> *I feel cross and ignored when you leave your clothes on the floor after I've asked you to pick them up. Please can you put them away this evening?*

Expressing yourself like this puts you in a powerful position and is more likely to give you the outcome you want, because you're:

- Expressing yourself honestly
- Not being accusing
- Making the conversation personal by telling the person you're talking to how you feel.

It's far harder for someone to argue with your feelings than with your opinions. They can spend all day disputing your opinion but they can't really contest the way you feel.

You may not want to communicate your own subtext if you're engaged in the tricky dynamics of political negotiation or professional poker but in most other situations communicating your own subtext creates new levels of honesty and a far better connection with people – it's another simple secret to having fulfilling conversations.

STEP 3:
Start Paying Attention to What People Aren't Saying

How do you know when there's a subtext to what someone's saying in a conversation? It's not an exact science, but if you use your intuition and pay attention to what the person may be *thinking* or *feeling*, rather than merely focusing on what they're saying, you can pick up some pretty strong clues.

If a sales manager says ,'We're behind on our numbers and there'll be hell to pay if we don't catch up,' she might actually mean, 'I'm *feeling* under pressure to hit my target.'

Or, if a child says, 'I don't really want to audition for the school play,' he might actually mean, 'I'm *worried* that I'm not good enough and I don't want to look like an idiot.'

And if politicians dodge questions during a TV debate, their subtext might be, 'I *can't admit* that I haven't got a solution to this crisis but I have to sound as if I've got a well-thought-out, clear and believable strategy and that I'm in command of the situation.'

If someone seems unusually defensive or says something out of character it's likely there's more to what they're saying than they're letting on. Using the same technique of inquiry introduced in Step 1 can help you uncover what it is. Knowing that conversations have different layers of meaning, and being able to get beneath the surface to identify them, will help you understand people better.

As they talk, people display all kinds of clues that point to what they really mean. Their intonation and body language, the ease – or otherwise – with which they're expressing themselves, the words they choose and the gaps and the silences they leave can all indicate how they're feeling. In order to avoid Mixed Messages, though, it's important to ask questions and then listen rather than simply try to guess what it is that someone might not be saying.

STEP 4:
Be Aware of Cultural Differences

When Mia and Ravi first got together, it took a while for Mia to become familiar with Ravi's family's customs. When his Indian parents nodded their heads, she initially took this as a sign of agreement but it didn't mean they were saying 'yes'; it meant, 'I'm listening to you.' They were offering empathy, but not necessarily approval or support.

Beth also had a lesson in cultural differences while on a six-month placement, teaching English in Shanghai. She was amazed at how highly she was regarded by her Chinese pupils and their parents; much more so than in the UK. However, whenever she and the headteacher met parents together, she felt offended that the parents seemed to ignore her. Eventually she understood that the headteacher's grey hair and greater experience meant that the parents listened more keenly to his words than to hers.

Once, during a conversation that Beth had with the parents of a student, the husband appeared to disagree with his wife. Beth noticed an involuntary reaction from her – she looked as though she'd just received an electric shock. Her Chinese friends explained afterwards what had happened. The concept of 'face' is very important in their society and is inextricably linked to one's standing and worth. The husband had displayed a lack of respect for his wife by disagreeing with her in public. In doing so, she had lost face, causing him also to lose face.

Beth's experience taught her that there are countless different cultural nuances that can appear in the subtext of a conversation, shaping people's behaviour. The best way of understanding these nuances is to ask for them to be explained to you.

Lesson 5: The issue you're discussing may not be the real issue.

CHAPTER SIX

LISTEN, DON'T PREPARE TO SPEAK
Why Shallow Listening Leads to Shallow Relationships

There's a peculiar practice called the filibuster that's sometimes used in parliamentary proceedings. It involves a member prolonging a debate for as long as necessary to prevent a particular vote being held. It's basically a time-wasting technique that was used back in ancient Rome and has perhaps been best exemplified more recently by two US senators.

In 1935 the Louisiana Democrat Huey Long spent over 15 hours telling stories about his uncle and explaining how to fry oysters while his fellow senators snored, buried themselves in a good novel or caught up on their admin.[1] Long later commented that he'd been 'in heaven discussing this thing', but his fellow senators certainly weren't in heaven and didn't notice any sign of discussion taking place either. When the call of nature finally compelled Long to dash to the men's room at 4am, his colleagues scurried into action and passed the bill he'd been trying to block.

Long's feat was topped by Strom Thurmond who, in 1957, managed to extend a monologue from 8.54pm on 28 August until 9.12pm on 29 August, all the while snacking on supplies of bread and sirloin steak. Thurmond became a legendary figure due to his unrivalled bladder control.

The word 'filibuster' has its roots in the Spanish word for 'freebooter' or 'pirate' – a filibuster is essentially a robber. We've all sat through lessons, lectures or meetings where it has felt as though we're enduring a Huey Long filibuster and are being robbed of time. Someone's speaking but nobody's listening.

I've experienced numerous youth football matches where the opposing team's coach has delivered a filibuster-type speech at a megaphonic level, lasting from kick-off to the final whistle. The players on his team invariably ignore him. Similarly, it's all too easy for parents to fall into filibuster mode; talking without paying careful attention to whether or not they're being listened to, and not listening themselves to what anyone says to them. However well intended, what we might think of as being helpful advice can sound like a stream of white noise.

THE SPECTRUM OF LISTENING

Often, the problem stems from conversational traffic being one-way only. Human beings are social creatures, and being social is a two-way process. Being talked at feels anti-social; we need to listen because we all know what it's like not to be listened to. The act of listening can be a tricky thing to define, but let's make three distinctions to create a spectrum.

[1] **Pretending to listen** – We're perfectly capable of sitting in front of someone and appearing to be attentive. I can nod my head at the right moments to make you think I'm listening, while actually I'm thinking about anything from dinner this evening to how I'm going to handle my next meeting, without hearing a word you're saying. My pretence might fall apart if you ask me to repeat what you've just said, or seek my opinion on the matter, but even then I could ask you to clarify your last point and buy myself some time in which to tune in. The art of pretending to listen without actually listening can be a useful device, but it's not conducive to healthy conversation.

In a similar vein, have you ever met someone for the first time whose name you struggled to remember moments after you first introduced yourselves to one another? They told you their name and you told them yours. As you shook hands, saying 'good to meet you', you could have sworn you heard what they said, but now you don't seem to be able to remember whether they're Liz, Margaret or Jemima.

You simply weren't listening, without even consciously realizing it. There are numerous occasions when our attention is occupied elsewhere. In these moments of distraction we can safely say there's no listening going on in the conversational equation.

[2] **'Normal' listening** – We like to think that conversations consist of one person speaking and the other person listening. However, the reality is a bit different. Let's take the example of Ravi and Mia. They're having a conversation about their plans for the weekend. It's not an argument, but they do have a habit of interrupting and finishing one another's sentences.

It happens like this: while Ravi is speaking, Mia is preparing to speak. Then Mia cuts in and becomes the speaker while Ravi prepares to speak. Then he jumps in when he thinks it's his turn, and Mia reverts to preparing to speak. The conversation trundles along like this, raising the question, 'Exactly who is doing the listening?'

Of course, both of them are listening to a degree, but it's pretty shallow and when listening is shallow relationships tend to be shallow, too. If this way of conducting their conversations is their predominant conversational modus operandi it will limit their ability to achieve depth in their relationship.

The following are two examples of shallow or normal listening:

[a] **Listening in order to confirm a pre-formed point of view** – The human brain is capable of receiving huge amounts of information every second but there's no way it can actually process such quantities of raw data. To do that, we'd need to have brains so incredibly large that our spines – as they are – wouldn't be able to support the weight. A brilliant solution is

to rely on stored perceptions of the world so the brain doesn't have to re-evaluate it constantly. Think of it like a cache system on a computer: by storing certain bits of data, the computer can retrieve information more quickly than if it has to search for it afresh.

Unfortunately, there's a downside to this solution. We'll develop a point of view based on the brain's stored perceptions and then listen *through* that view.

A friend told me a poignant story that illustrates this. Whenever his teenage son wanted to borrow money from him he'd say, 'Dad …?' with a similar tone, in a particular way. It got so familiar that he immediately knew that a request for money was going to follow – or so he thought. On one occasion, when his son approached him in the same way, Dad frowned and rolled his eyes. Straight away, his son muttered, 'Forget it,' and slunk off. Later that evening, the father had the presence of mind to ask his son what he'd been about to say. His reply was, 'I wanted you to know that I'd had a terrible day at school.'

How much of life do we miss because we're busy confirming the subjective perceptions that we've established as points of view? It's much easier to confirm an opinion than to question it – especially with the people closest to us.

[b] Self-referential listening – A man meets a woman at a party and they strike up a conversation. Whenever it starts to wander off in another direction the man brings it back to himself. Toward the end of the evening he says, 'Listen, I'm really sorry, I've spent the whole time talking about me. Let's talk about you now.' The woman breathes a sigh of relief. 'So,' he continues, 'what do *you* think about *me*?'

This little story is a perfect example of self-referential listening. We all do it. We love to steer a conversation onto our own track so we can share our experience, and offer our opinions and advice. When two or more people are in this mode, it quickly leads to Dominatricks, which will disrupt the conversation's flow and rhythm.

The root of the word 'discussion' aptly means 'to smash apart, scatter or disperse', and a lot of conversations conform to this definition. A supposedly straightforward topic becomes frustratingly hard and complicated, seeming to involve a repetitive process of breaking up and piecing back together again. It's not necessarily a problem if you're having a chat over a pint of beer, but it can quickly become one if there's a battle of wills going on in a work meeting.

If we imagine the act of listening as the potential to immerse ourselves in a vast ocean, I'd argue that we generally only tend to paddle up to our ankles. This is fine at a transactional level – if you're looking for the nearest bank and someone tells you to turn right then first left, you'll still get your needs met. However, there's a price to pay if you consistently listen in this way.

If you always remain in the shallows with those you're close to, they probably won't bother to bring up issues for fear of being judged rather than heard. And your partner won't voice any deeper concerns about your relationship for fear it'll spark yet another damaging row. These are exactly the situations in which it's vital to wade out into that ocean and listen deeply. A 2013 Prince's Trust survey found that 22 per cent of young people in the UK felt they didn't have anyone to talk to about their problems while they were growing up.[2] Most of them surely had friends and family around them, but they didn't trust that they would be heard.

[3] Listening from nothing – There's a much deeper form of listening, which requires being fully present while the other person's speaking. It's not as easy as it sounds because we tend to spend a lot of our conversations being preoccupied with:

- Composing a brilliant reply
- Seeking to gain the upper hand
- Evaluating the merit of what the other person's saying
- Working out how to fix the problem that's being outlined to you
- Waiting for the other person to stop speaking so that you can speak.

I call the deeper form of listening 'listening from nothing', and it's very different to listening through your agenda. This doesn't mean that you have to surrender your opinions or become a passive participant in conversations. On the contrary, when you've given your complete attention to someone else's words as a precursor to speaking yourself, you're more likely to pick up both the content of the conversation and the emotions and values in its subtext. You'll be absorbed in the present moment rather than extrapolating ahead or rewinding your mental tape. Your responses will be more agile, sharper and attuned to the other person's perspective.

When you're on the receiving end of this deeper listening, you'll feel as if you're really being heard and that the person with whom you're speaking is connected with you and your world. Depending on who you're talking to, feelings of respect, profound affinity or love will be a natural consequence.

I was chatting about this approach to listening with a team of senior managers in South Africa. One of them, Philip, reflected on his own experience. He described the way his wife welcomed local kids and teenagers to their house. Philip had asked one of the teenagers why he chose to hang around at his place, instead of down at the football pitch with the other young people. The boy replied, 'I come to your house because your wife listens *as if I'm here*.'

It's worth reading that sentence several times. Personally, I'd benefit from keeping it in mind every day. It's got a haunting quality that nags at my conscience, and I can't help scanning through a mental list of my own friends and family – wondering how well I measure up.

When people reflect on the times in their lives when they've grown and flourished the most, they consistently report that a family member, colleague or friend 'listened as if they were there'. I know that at times I've been able to step up to the mark, but at others I've clearly failed. As the years have passed, I've concluded that this is one of the most critical legacies I'd wish to leave for my children. I'm aware that it can't be bought with money or favours. Instead, it will be the product of the many thousands of interactions I've had with them. However well I think I may have listened, they will be the judges of my success.

WHAT TO DO?

STEP 1:
Be In the Conversation You're In

Strive to be fully present in the conversation you're in, rather than being preoccupied with the last or next one. The truth is that you can only ever be in the one that you're in. As you switch from one to another, make a choice to be in it fully.

Just as a sports professional will never play to her highest potential in every match, it's impossible to achieve this in each and every interaction you have. But constant practice will enable you to demonstrate it more and more consistently.

STEP 2:
Bring Back Your Attention When It Drifts

When you start listening more attentively, it's likely you'll become acutely aware of the way your thoughts keep interrupting. It tends to work in the following way.

Mia and Ravi are discussing their son's teacher at school. Ravi's reply of 'Um, OK then,' masks the chatter in his head, which is going something like:

> Yes … fair enough … what time is it? I've got to reply to that email by 5 o'clock … OK, I've got your point … I forgot to call the electrician yesterday … I wonder who that missed call was from …

Ravi experiences a constant stream of mind chatter that is either past-based ('I forgot to call the electrician yesterday') or future-based ('I've got to reply to that email by 5 o'clock'). There are times when this running commentary seems to swamp his consciousness and he can't switch it off. The best he can aim for is to keep noticing when his attention drifts away and to bring it back to the conversation he's involved with in that moment. If he can do this more consistently, the quality of his interactions will go up exponentially.

Try practising this in every single conversation you have, every day. And, if sometimes you don't have the headspace to do it, you have the option to say, 'I'm really sorry, can we talk about this later when I can listen to you properly?'

Surely, it's more respectful and effective than casually going through the motions.

STEP 3:
Allow Pauses

Gaps and pauses during a conversation can feel uncomfortable. Our inclination is to fill them, even if it means talking rubbish. Moving away from the shores of shallow listening into the depths requires giving people space to finish a sentence and giving enough of a pause to allow them to hear, in their own mind, what they've just said. I never cease to marvel at the difference this can make.

Someone might say, 'There's absolutely nothing I can do about my situation at work.' If I remember to hold back and not jump in at the end of their sentence, after a few moments of silence they may continue: 'Well, of course, that's not entirely true … I could look for another job … Or I suppose I could speak to my manager … I'm not sure he'll listen … Then again, I don't have much to lose if it goes wrong …' These moments of silence often allow people to voice their deeper feelings and concerns, and reach their own solutions.

Perhaps the greatest contribution you can provide is to be fully present; allowing the person you're speaking with the time and space to become clear about how they feel, what they really think and how they wish to move forward. Sometimes the real action in a conversation takes place in the pauses, when nothing at all is being said.

Lesson 6: Sometimes the most powerful thing you can provide is silence.

CHAPTER SEVEN

LEAN INTO YOUR THOUGHTS AND FEELINGS
How to Deal with Negative Thoughts and Feelings

Despite what the characters might have you believe, in a Punch and Judy show it's not the puppets that are running things. Even though they're behind the curtain, it's the puppeteers who pull the strings. Similarly, thoughts and feelings can dominate how we conduct a conversation.

If you think you have nothing to contribute, you'll more than likely keep your mouth shut. If you feel exasperated, the tone of your discussion will probably be affected. If you think you can't trust someone, then you'll be selective about what you reveal. We don't actually choose our thoughts and feelings, and this has worrying implications. I'll give you an example.

If you were told with only an hour's notice that you had to speak in front of a crowd of 10,000 people, would you make the decision to feel scared or would you feel scared anyway? For the vast majority of us, it would be the latter. Would you purposely fill your head with nightmarish thoughts about how you'll freeze under the spotlight and wind up looking ridiculous? I don't think any of us would choose to be apprehensive, afraid and uncomfortable, but in certain situations our thoughts and feelings are triggered spontaneously. Interestingly, in research polls the fear of public speaking actually scores higher than the fear of death.

Thoughts and feelings come and go and it's up to us to distinguish which ones we pay attention to. Like Dame Judi Dench, it *is* possible to use them to our advantage. She claims that the more she acts the more frightened she becomes. Yet she's received one Oscar, two Golden Globes and 10 BAFTA awards. Such was the force of her performance in the film *Shakespeare in Love* that she won her Oscar despite being onscreen for only nine minutes.

In contrast to thousands of aspiring performers across the world who are waiting for the day when they'll overcome their fear, Dame Judi sees her fear as being vital to her success. She understands that the battle to suppress or banish negative feelings simply can't be won. 'I have the fear,' she says. 'I wouldn't be without it.'

To her it's more of an accepted and appreciated companion than an enemy because, most importantly, she's found a way to *have* her fear rather than to *be* it.

DEALING WITH YOUR THOUGHTS

On the subject of public speaking, I met a man who arrived at the same realization as Judi Dench and it transformed his life. George grew up with an absolute fear of speaking in front of large groups. Even in work meetings, with a dozen-or-so people, he'd keep his thoughts to himself. Over the years, he'd become involved in trade union organizations and was a regular attendee at their conferences. At one particular meeting, which had about 4,000 attendees, the woman leading it asked George if he'd deliver the closing speech on the following day. The idea seemed absurd to him. More than absurd – George felt physically sick at the thought.

However, the woman was very convincing. She pointed out to George that she was accountable for the success of the conference, and that she trusted him implicitly. She told him that he had something valuable to contribute. George knew this much was true.

After a lengthy conversation, and much to his own astonishment, he agreed to do it. He woke during the early hours of the following day in a panic. His negative thoughts were on the rampage, telling him: 'George, this is the greatest mistake you have ever made in your life. You're going to make a complete idiot of yourself. Today will ruin your career, and your reputation will be on the scrapheap.'

But George didn't want to let his friend down. He had agreed to make the closing speech, and his friend was relying on him and must have believed that he could do it. Before the time came, he went for a long walk along the pier, breathing in the fresh sea air and gathering himself together before walking into the conference hall and delivering his speech. As he finished, 4,000 people stood up to give him a standing ovation. He now speaks at conferences the world over.

What happened? George realized that he could have all his negative thoughts and feelings and still get up and speak – just as Judi Dench can feel terrified and still deliver award-winning performances. This has significant implications if we apply it across all areas of life. It means we can be scared and speak up, or concerned about challenging someone and still raise our concerns. Above all, it shows that it is possible to own our thoughts and feelings rather than being owned by them.

GET BACK TO CHOICE

George's story echoes my own. As a young boy I went to school hundreds – and, at times, thousands – of miles from home. I felt I had to stuff my feelings into a dark corner of my being in order to be able to cope with the business of daily life. However, this strategy was relatively unsuccessful. I suppressed my feelings at times when I would have benefited from expressing them and they'd spill out when I wished I could shut the lid on them. I realized early on that dealing with feelings is a precarious business.

I can remember being in social situations as a teenager, wishing that I was invisible. Tongue-tied at the time, I'd be racked with self-reproach afterwards.

When I felt especially self-conscious, my face would go a deep shade of red. The more I sought to avoid this happening, the more it seemed to occur – proving that 'what you resist persists'. It was only when I was in my 20s that I realized that it's possible to feel embarrassed and still fully participate in a conversation – that they aren't mutually exclusive.

It would seem extraordinary to my teenage persona that I've spent the majority of my adult life speaking in public forums. On the occasions when this has involved talking in front of hundreds of people my nerves are the same – I've just learned to accept them. Since the physiological expressions of anxiety and excitement are largely the same, such as a raised heartbeat and sweaty palms, it's hard to know which I'm feeling. Over time, I've learned to accept that my thoughts and feelings can be highly paradoxical. It's perfectly possible to feel thankful and guilty, exasperated and determined, hopeful and discouraged, irritated and concerned – *all at the same time.*

These contrasts are the reality of our human experience, whatever our background and walk of life; we just need to accept this, and learn to live with the inconsistencies that our thoughts and feelings seem to throw up.

WHY WE TRIP UP

Beth learns this the hard way when she goes for an interview for the role of deputy head at a primary school. It includes meeting a panel of the school's governors. It's an intimidating process but everything seems to be going well until someone asks a particularly difficult question. It's a seminal moment, after which Beth's performance and prospects seem to spiral downward. On closer inspection, the trigger for Beth's problem is not the difficult question but a series of private thoughts that she treats as statements of truth, tipping her into the Bad Place.

Here's the conversation (Beth's thoughts are in the lightly shaded boxes):

What would you do if a teaching assistant came to you voicing concerns about a teacher's ability to keep control of the class?

Well, um … I'd want to meet with the teacher and see how they think things are going.

Are you sure? Wouldn't you want to discuss it with the head first, or observe part of a lesson before approaching the teacher directly?

Oh, yes … well, of course, I'd do that as well.

That was horrible. He's going to think I'm useless now. I totally blew that.

OK. So how would you go about it?

Um, well … obviously … as you said, I'd let the headteacher know that a concern had been raised, but I'd also want to check the facts in more detail.

That was even worse. I can't believe this is happening. Now he's glaring at me.

How exactly would you check the facts?

I'm sorry; could you repeat the question please?

I wish the floor would swallow me up.

After Beth notices that the governor is frowning and starts thinking that she's blown her chances, a series of chemical reactions are triggered in her body, known as a 'stress response'. In the face of this, she is struggling to maintain her focus and has mentally lost her centre of gravity. The irony of the situation is that the governor was actually rather impressed with Beth up to this point. Beth's negative bias has kicked in, telling her that she's failing the interview. She takes this thought on board, as if it's the truth of the situation, and it sends her overall performance downhill.

The point is that our thoughts are not necessarily true – as Ethan found out after he'd concluded that he was going to lose his job at his bank. Beth needs to realize that her internal dialogue can get loud and negative. She has to be able to notice it chattering away, but not get tangled up in it. It's no different to the situation of the professional tennis player whose game is guaranteed to suffer because she gets caught up in thinking about the volley she missed in the last game rather than playing the point in front of her.

Beth attaches significance to her thoughts and feelings and ends up getting swamped by them, rather than being able to hold the truth lightly. This dictates her mental state and subsequent responses.

What's the alternative? Ideally, Beth would have noticed her thoughts and feelings in much the same way as you might notice a cloud drifting across the sky on a breezy afternoon. When this happens, you don't make the cloud have any significance in relation to your worth and value. The cloud doesn't make you a lesser or a greater person. Similarly, Beth could have noticed the thought:

> *That was even worse. I can't believe this is happening. Now he's glaring at me.*

To be able to do this successfully, she won't attach any significance to her thought. She'll remember that it isn't necessarily true. It'll jump into her consciousness but she'll swiftly bring her attention back to the question that the governor is asking her. In a moment or so, it will disappear, to be replaced by another thought. She'll know that some of her thoughts will be positive and others intensely negative, and she'll let them go in order to stay focused on what's happening in the room, rather than following what's in her head.

If Beth is able to apply this under pressure during an interview, she'll be able to apply it across her life. When Dan, her partner, doesn't notice that she's had her hair highlighted, her negative thoughts kick in and she feels irritated. But if she is able to *notice* her thoughts and feelings, she doesn't have to be subject to them, like a puppet on a string. Of course, this doesn't mean she's gagged and can't express herself to Dan. Rather, she'll be able to stop and think about how she wants to express herself rather than firing off a shotgun response that sparks the Big Argument but feels in hindsight like a bit of an overreaction.

WHAT TO DO?

STEP 1:
Notice Your Thoughts and Feelings

Remember that the thoughts and feelings you have in any situation may have nothing to do with your commitments in that moment. The greatest achievements in your life may have been preceded or accompanied by feelings of terror, concern, frustration or anxiety, but you still went ahead.

A thought or feeling in itself doesn't prevent you from taking any action. It's easy to think, 'I'm frightened and can't speak.' This is a trick of the mind. It would be more accurate and authentic to say, 'I'm frightened and I'm choosing not to speak.' When you do so, you become the author of your decision rather than a victim of circumstance.

Negative thoughts and feelings do serve a purpose. If you feel frustrated with someone, your frustration is telling you that you care about something. If you're walking home late at night and see someone who you think might be following you, your fear puts you on the alert. However, in a lot of situations, your thoughts and feelings won't be aligned with your values and commitments and so may not be dependable signposts for action.

STEP 2:
Identify Your Commitments

Since thoughts and feelings can be an unreliable compass when it comes to making decisions, it's worth asking what you're really committed to. This will provide a more solid base for action.

Look at the following list. Reading from left to right, what's the most reliable basis for making a decision and taking action in each situation? Is it your thoughts, your feelings or your commitments?

THOUGHTS	FEELINGS	COMMITMENTS
I can't raise the issue. It will wreck our relationship.	Anxiety	To have an open and honest relationship
I'm going to hit a bad note and look like a loser.	Fear	To play in the orchestra to the best of my ability
I'm never going to pass my exam. It's hopeless.	Resignation	To get my professional qualification
You're being outrageously inconsiderate.	Anger	To resolve our differences

In each case, you'd respond differently if you based your actions on your commitments rather than on your thoughts and feelings. In practice this might mean that you speak up rather than withholding your anger and feeling resentful, or listen when you'd rather be wedded to your point of view. It's not always easy to act in line with our commitments, but when we manage to do so we're usually being true to our longer-term aims and underlying values.

STEP 3:
Express and Acknowledge Feelings

As Lara found with young Jack and Anna with regards to their untidy rooms, expressing your feelings is likely to have a more positive impact than venting your opinions. To communicate your feelings, you'll need to pause for a second to identify what they are; they may not come immediately to mind. When you do this, you may find that you have a bundle of feelings rather than one.

Having and expressing your feelings is very different from allowing them to take over. People who *are* their feelings are prone to lash out, verbally or physically, when they feel intensely angry and frustrated. This is often the source of violent and abusive behaviour.

The other side to expressing feelings is to acknowledge them. If you're fizzing with anger on the end of a phone, a highly skilled customer service representative will start by acknowledging your feelings. They may respond with: 'I'm sorry; this must be very frustrating and disappointing for you.' Met with this response, you'll probably feel the frustration drain away, leaving you able to engage in a pragmatic conversation, rather than still wanting to bark at them. On the other hand, if someone fails to listen and simply attempts to justify their position, your frustration levels may rise to boiling point and pour out in an angry tirade.

STEP 4:
Challenging your Truth and Logic

The ability of athletes to deal with negative emotions while under immense physical strain and mental pressure is a decisive ingredient for success. Dr Steve Peters is the psychiatrist behind the Olympic British Cycling Team and Team Sky ProCycling. In his book *The Chimp Paradox* he reinforces the importance of being able to express our thoughts and feelings to someone who will 'listen from nothing', without attaching any significance to them, getting offended or jumping in with their judgments.

Whether it's Lara expressing her emotions to Ethan or an Olympic athlete doing so before the race of his life, there's no substitute for being heard in this way. In the process, a transformation can take place; our thinking becomes less rigid and more malleable, meaning that we can challenge the truth and logic of what we're saying. Rather than seeing the world in black and white, we can start to see the grey. When this happens, we discover that we don't have to be dominated by our thoughts and feelings. Rather than having the awful experience that they are running amok and ruining our life, we can let them come and go and yet keep our focus on what's important to us.

Lesson 7: Allow your thoughts and feelings but base your actions on your values and commitments.

CHAPTER
EIGHT

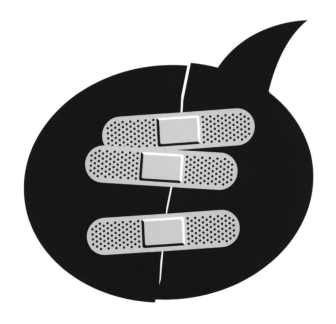

STOP FIXING PEOPLE'S PROBLEMS
Why People Don't Want Your Advice and What They Want Instead

One of the most prolific writers in English history on the fine art of becoming a gentleman was the Earl of Chesterfield. His letters on the subject, each of which starts with the words 'Dear Boy', were so extensive that he makes Leo Tolstoy look like a short-story writer. The recipient of his letters was his illegitimate son Philip Stanhope, who was attending Westminster School at the time. Little did Philip realize when he received the first letter, dated 9 October 1746, that another 99 would follow – each stuffed to the gunnels with advice.

The earl had much to say about conversation. 'Never think of entertaining people with your own personal concerns or private affairs; though they are interesting to you, they are tedious and impertinent to everybody else; besides that, one cannot keep one's own private affairs too secret.' [1]

His son seemed to take these words to heart because soon after the young man's premature death, the earl received correspondence from a woman explaining that she was the penniless mother of two young boys, and that he was their grandfather. However, much of the earl's advice was lost in the wind, due to its overwhelming volume. If he'd known that it's better not to offer advice unless it's been asked for he could have saved himself vast quantities of time, effort and ink.

THE ADDICTED ADVICE-GIVER

Even if advice is asked or paid for, it doesn't necessary mean that it will work. Tim Gallwey discovered this in the 1970s. He described how, as a newly qualified professional tennis coach, he would give careful and well-intended advice to eager tennis students. After a series of instructions, a student's head would be whirling with information, to the point where he could barely see the ball. Progress seemed to be slow and complicated.

Gallwey became dissatisfied with his teaching methods and the progress of his students and started to focus on what he called the 'inner game' of tennis. He'd noticed that verbal instructions often *decreased* rather than *increased* the probability of someone improving their game. As a result, he broke away from traditional methods of sports coaching, vowing never to offer advice. Since then he's coached world champions. How can this be?

Gallwey realized that if he encouraged students to observe how they were playing their shots, without judging themselves for how they were playing, their game immediately improved. Rather than telling a student: 'You need to roll your wrist on the backhand,' Gallwey's approach encouraged students to volunteer, 'I notice that I don't roll my wrist on my backhand.' Gallwey sparked a 30-year revolution in sports coaching that continues to this day. The best youth coaches the world over are now trained to limit the advice they give and instead ask questions that allow people to let go of self-judgments, focus on what is happening and trust their natural learning process.

When I experienced Tim's approach first-hand I made more progress on my backhand in an hour than in my previous 30 years of tennis, and without a single word of advice. This was a humbling experience. It forced me to call into question the incessant need I had to offer people advice, tips and solutions. I'd argue that this very common trait is probably the biggest handicap to effective practice for managers, parents, partners, teachers and … well, all of us.

RATTLING AROUND IN THE HOUSE

Ethan, our corporate banker, has the following conversation with his mum, Lily. It doesn't go disastrously wrong, but it doesn't seem to go that well either:

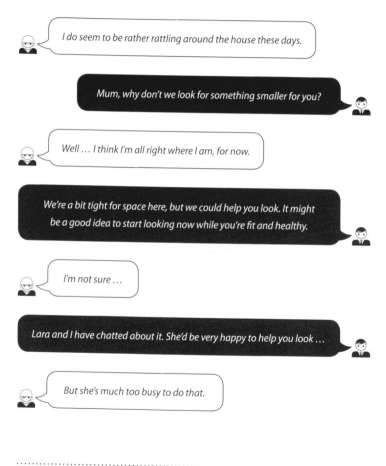

I do seem to be rather rattling around the house these days.

Mum, why don't we look for something smaller for you?

Well … I think I'm all right where I am, for now.

We're a bit tight for space here, but we could help you look. It might be a good idea to start looking now while you're fit and healthy.

I'm not sure …

Lara and I have chatted about it. She'd be very happy to help you look …

But she's much too busy to do that.

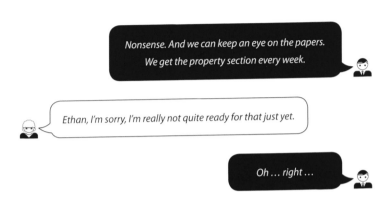

Nonsense. And we can keep an eye on the papers. We get the property section every week.

Ethan, I'm sorry, I'm really not quite ready for that just yet.

Oh ... right ...

Later than evening, Ethan says to Lara, 'Mum complained that she was rattling around in her house and when I suggested moving somewhere smaller she got totally defensive. I was only trying to help.' When Lily goes home that evening, she thinks, 'That was odd. It felt like Ethan was trying to push me out of my house.'

Ethan used his mother's opening comment as a cue to solve what he identified as a problem. The real question is: what's the problem and whose problem is it? The answer's not as straightforward as you might think at first glance.

Lily *doesn't* have a problem with her house. She's merely making a throwaway comment and expressing how she feels. She's happy in her house and has lots of memories associated with it. On the other hand, Ethan does have a problem. He's concerned about what the future holds for his mother, and that she doesn't wait too long to downsize. Under scrutiny it's apparent that the problem is actually *his*. Another way of putting this would be to say that he's offering a solution to a problem that's worrying him and that he thinks his mother *ought* to be worried about, too. When looked at in this way, it's clear why Lily's not very receptive to Ethan's suggestions.

If Lily does have a problem, it's that she's quite lonely and doesn't see as much of Ethan, Lara and their kids as she'd like. But Ethan takes her comment literally and now they're in the Tangle.

There are a lot of managers who tend to act in the same way as Ethan. They believe that they're not worth their salt unless they're analysing and fixing problems, and it's through their apparent ability to do this that they judge their sense of self-worth. But there are downsides:

- It can become wearing for the people they manage, and also relatively disempowering; they're not encouraged to develop problem-solving skills by resolving issues for themselves.
- They get so addicted to fixing 'problems' that it's hard for them to change gear when they get home. Partners and children don't respond kindly to this approach and usually don't hesitate to say so.

WHAT TO DO?

STEP 1:
Give Space, Not Solutions

More often than not, someone will raise an issue because they want to be heard rather than have it fixed. The extent to which men tend to do this drives women mad. Though there is a gender bias toward the incidence of this annoying habit, it's not exclusive to men. The fact is that people of both sexes want to be heard. They want others to understand how they're feeling and to have their personal experience acknowledged and validated.

By asking a few questions and listening, without going into solution mode, Ethan would be able to identify clearly what his mother means:

 I do seem to be rather rattling around the house these days.

What do you mean, Mum?

 Well, I keep busy and active but it's obviously not been the same since I've been living on my own. I'm fine in myself, though.

It must be quite lonely at times. Is it?

 I don't want to complain. I suppose it is, but you get used to it.

When you say you're rattling around, is that because the house is too big?

 It probably is a bit big for me now. But I love it and I don't want to let it go just yet. We've had such happy times there. It keeps me going really – if that makes any sense.

Conversations get so much richer when we give them space. Ethan now has a completely different understanding of what his mother really means. Moreover, because he's actually listening she's able to reveal more about herself and her feelings. In this context it becomes obvious that the solution isn't to look for a smaller house in the local newspaper's property pages.

STEP 2:
Give Advice When Requested

It's usually best to follow the general rule not to offer advice unless it's been requested. If you work on an IT help desk, in a consumer advice bureau, or in a specialist consulting company, you're paid for your expertise. You'll need to advise people as comprehensively as you're able. But when you go home and give advice to your daughter, you need to clock whether or not she's actually asked for it. If she hasn't, at best you're likely to get a Yes, But … response to your suggestions. More likely, though, is that she'll turn off and zone out. When she sees her friends she'll probably tell them her parents are always nagging her.

It might be difficult to accept that unsolicited advice is generally ignored so of no value, but this is indeed the case. Despite this, I often find that I can't help myself. When my son goes off to a school sports match, I feel compelled to offer last-minute tips before he goes. It probably makes me feel better for having said it but the chances are that he, or whoever's on the receiving end, will ignore it.

STEP 3:
Ask What People Need – and Say What You Need, Too

People tend to be very unclear about what they need from someone in a conversation. They might say, 'I'm really having problems with Dave at work,' without giving any indication as to whether they're just passing the time of day or whether they want you to listen, help them get clear, offer your opinion or fix the problem. In all probability they may not know themselves.

It doesn't do any harm to listen and ask questions in order to get a fuller understanding of what they're saying. You can also ask them what they need. If they say, 'I don't think I need anything,' this is your cue to keep your wisdom to yourself – even though you might find it desperately hard to suppress. On the other hand, if they say, 'It would be good to get your advice,' this is like getting the winning numbers on a lottery ticket – inviting you to launch in with your suggestions. Like the parable of the farmer who sows his seed on fertile rather than stony ground, there's a far greater probability that your input will make a difference if it's been asked for.

There's another way of testing whether your advice might make a difference. Try offering a pearl of wisdom and listen to what you get back. If you get a Yes, But … response it's a good indication that your advice isn't wanted. Go back to listening and asking questions; find another way to support the person you're having a conversation with, though simply listening is often enough.

STEP 4:
Ask Thoughtful Questions

Asking questions is an art in itself. Voltaire got it right when he said, 'Judge a man by his questions rather than by his answers.' It requires being able to place yourself in the other person's world and to consider what might help facilitate their thought process.

Great leaders and managers focus on the questions they're going to ask rather than the advice they're burning to give. This isn't to say that advice can't be given, but it's best used sparingly and with discretion.

I remember a performance appraisal I had, years ago, during which, and over lunch, my manager asked me how I'd evaluate my year. He went on to ask what motivated me, what was next on my agenda, how I thought I could build on my strengths and what I needed from him. It was like being in a tennis lesson with Tim Gallwey. He did give a light sprinkling of input, but the ratio of speaking was at least 80:20 in my favour. It was conducted so well that, nearly 20 years later, it still sticks in my mind. Most appraisals had little impact and have long receded into an unmemorable blur.

Lesson 8: Most advice just sounds like noise.

CHAPTER
NINE

CHANGE YOUR PERSPECTIVE
How to Resolve Issues by Taking a Different Vantage Point

Look at the circles marked A and B below. Which is larger? It seems blindingly obvious that the answer is B. Actually, the two circles are identical in size.[1] To accept this fact, you may need to measure them.

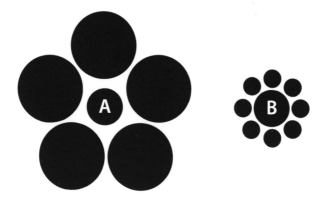

What we see and hear doesn't always match with reality. The problem is that we see life through our own narrow lens. Conversations can either follow a predictable path in which we trade myopic beliefs with glorious self-righteousness or we can ask people for help in seeing the view from their vantage point, reshaping our convictions in the process. This requires a willingness to be curious.

AM I BEING NARROW-MINDED?
While researching a book about a school for trainers of exotic animals, journalist and author Amy Sutherland took the concept of the alternative

perspective to radical lengths.[2] Having spent years trying to turn her husband Scott into her ideal partner, she'd reached the conclusion that her strategy of nagging only made things worse. Rather than resigning herself to irritation, she decided to test the trainers' techniques on her husband.

For her particular experiment, Amy adopted the animal trainer's tried-and-tested practice of rewarding behaviour that you like and ignoring behaviour that you don't. In an article in the *New York Times*, she described how she started thanking Scott if he threw one dirty shirt into the laundry basket and kissing him if he threw in two. At the same time, she lured him away from behaviours she didn't like by coming up with attractive alternatives – when she didn't want him crowding her she'd put salsa and chips on the other side of the kitchen. And finally, she adopted the technique she'd seen the trainers use when an animal did something wrong – they didn't respond at all, following the principle that if a behaviour doesn't illicit a response, it tends to die away.

To Amy's surprise, each of these approaches worked as well on Scott as on the animals they'd been designed for. More importantly, the experiment forced her to question the view she had of her relationship. Rather than blaming Scott for failed training attempts, she looked for new strategies. The point is that she changed her perspective and, as a result, stopped having so many Blamestorming conversations.

We're all prone to sticking to die-hard routines, even when they don't work. It takes a lot less thought and effort than it does to make a difficult change. It's a bit like the man who tells his doctor that each time he has a cup of tea he gets a pain in the eye, so the doctor tells him to take the spoon out. Even when we know how to remove the source of our discomfort, it doesn't mean we'll do it – that requires effort and discipline. As a consequence, we're liable to repeat our bad habits; including our bad conversational habits, falling into the same holes and winding up in the same kind of arguments.

ADOPTING SECOND AND THIRD PERSPECTIVES

Ravi has a bad conversation about homework with Jay, his 10-year-old. Having been brought up to think that television's essentially a waste of time, and that people should be doing something more worthwhile, Ravi struggles with his children watching more than just a small amount. He gets especially grumpy about the programmes on the kids' channels, thinking they're banal and pointless.

Ravi is also tired and, in this situation, moves quickly from telling to moralizing and then threatening.

Come on, Jay, it's time to turn the TV off now and get on with your homework.

But the programme's nearly finished – it's only got 15 minutes to go.

It's a school night and you've been watching it for over an hour. You're becoming a TV junkie – you'll get square eyes.

I'm doing my French revision while I'm watching.

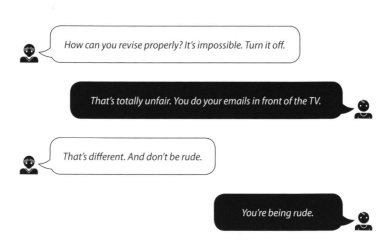

How can you revise properly? It's impossible. Turn it off.

That's totally unfair. You do your emails in front of the TV.

That's different. And don't be rude.

You're being rude.

With each comment, the volume and intensity of the conversation starts to increase. The warning lights are flashing and it's moving into Escalation. Ravi and Jay both have weapons in their armouries that they're ready to use – Ravi with the clear advantage in terms of being able to pull rank and Jay with the ability to manipulate his father emotionally.

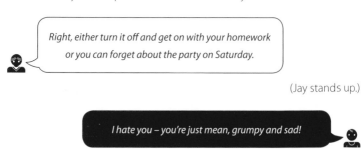

Right, either turn it off and get on with your homework or you can forget about the party on Saturday.

(Jay stands up.)

I hate you – you're just mean, grumpy and sad!

(He leaves the room, slamming the door.)

Jay eventually does his homework, but he won't speak to Ravi and it spoils the atmosphere in the house. It's only at bedtime that they patch things up. To make things worse, Mia tells Ravi that he's being too hard on Jay. She and Ravi end up having an argument.

It would help if Ravi was able to take a second and third perspective. The second perspective involves Ravi putting himself in Jay's shoes for a moment. He may not get it exactly right, and he won't necessarily agree with it, but it may go something like this:

> *I'm at school all week and I don't get much time to do what I want. You're on my case all the time. You don't understand what it's like for me; you keep talking about how it was for you at school but that was centuries ago. I'm tired; you make it sound like I don't do any work but that's unfair. You're working most of the week and don't know what I'm doing anyway. At least I do my homework – you don't know how lucky you are. I know you think the kids' channel is rubbish but I quite enjoy it.*

Ravi could also consider a third perspective. This would be the perspective of someone watching the conversation as an independent observer who has no personal agenda to push and no vested interest in the outcome. This would work best if Ravi envisaged someone whose balanced opinion he'd respect – his grandmother, for example. She always seemed to have a wise word and a level head and could be honest without making him feel that he was wrong. What would she have said? He can almost hear her voice and picture her face as she speaks.

> *Ravi, it sounds as though you feel Jay's wasting his time because watching TV is not something you value; you need to remember he's 10. You sound tired; you're in Blamestorming mode with him, but you'd be better off telling him how you feel and negotiating a solution together.*

Taking the second and third perspectives doesn't mean Ravi has to sit down with a piece of paper and write it all out. We're quite capable of considering different perspectives at the same time; just as we can safely drive a car while talking to a passenger, taking note of road signs, watching the speed limit and keeping an eye out for other vehicles.

The thing to remember is that the first, second and third perspectives are only perspectives – none of these viewpoints has a monopoly on the truth. When confronted by a disagreement our attitudes tend to become fixed, at precisely the moment when we'd benefit from being flexible. It will seem as if the first perspective is the most accurate because it's our own. But Ravi would do well to remember that he's in his living room, not a courtroom; he doesn't need to argue over 'the truth', even though his 10-year-old is making a valiant effort to do so. Neither does Ravi need to stamp his authority on the situation, which is his instinctive response when he's tired.

Having considered the second and third perspectives, Ravi can tackle the conversation in a different way and with a different tone – without making threats or moralizing. A response like the following one from Ravi won't make Jay jump for joy, but it does take his son's needs into account and is a reasonable proposal:

> *Jay, I know you need a break after a full day at school and I don't want to cut your programme off suddenly. Can we agree to turn it off in 15 minutes, at 7pm? If it hasn't finished, you could record it and watch the end after you've done your homework.*

The crucial ingredient is that Ravi isn't enforcing a control-based strategy. Efforts to exercise control almost always provoke either grudging compliance or resistance. By pausing for a moment to think about your approach to a conversation, angst can be avoided without any loss of authority. Rather than seeing situations in one dimension, adopting a second and third perspective provides you with a 3D view. In the process, it allows you to see different solutions.

In the heat of a flare-up it's all too easy to forget that the most powerful and fulfilling conversations involve people sharing and examining their stories in a spirit of exchange and understanding – even if they have very different world views. More often than not, this spirit leads to the creation of new and deeper levels of shared meaning.

WHAT TO DO?

STEP 1:
Get on Their Track

Understanding someone else's perspective begins with being curious and willing to ask questions and then listening. Your questions shouldn't be random but should encourage the other person to reflect on their experience. While doing this, it's important not to keep trying to bring the conversation back onto *your* track. Rather, keep it on their track and see what transpires.

STEP 2:
Imagine a Different Physical Position

While adopting the second perspective, make an effort to imagine yourself physically in the other person's position, looking at you. In the same way, when considering the third perspective, imagine yourself physically occupying the space between you and the other person. Doing so makes it easier to step out of your own mental world and consider a different stance.

STEP 3:
Drop Your Strategies for Control

It's a fact of life that we operate in hierarchies. At work, there are lines of accountability that describe who reports to whom, and even the CEO is accountable to others – whether customers, shareholders or the board of directors. In family life, there's also a degree of seniority and authority that comes with being the parent.

However, it's self-evident that managers and parents who persistently adopt strategies based on Dominatricks or Blamestorming – endlessly lecturing, moralizing or issuing threats – are largely ignored. Think about a teacher who is over-reliant on barking orders at their pupils in class. Ironically, because they command little respect, their authority is undermined. No longer able to bank on the goodwill of their students, they pull rank because it's the easiest option and because they don't have any other strings to pull. Getting the balance right is tricky, since the converse problem is not to exert any authority and to allow people to run riot around you. The moral seems to be that you can exert authority, and even hold people to account, without being belittling or overly controlling.

Generating trust clearly offers the most mileage in terms of getting the best from others, but it is hard won and easily lost. Genuinely seeking to understand another person's perspective doesn't imply that we need to take the soft option and surrender to their needs. Which of these would you rather experience: that someone more 'senior' to you took the time and trouble to adopt the second and third perspectives, then explained their decision and their reasons behind it; or that they ignored your opinion and simply told you what to do? We can put up with the latter once or twice, but it wears thin very quickly. In contrast, if someone makes genuine efforts to understand our perspective, there's a greater probability that a way forward will be found that's acceptable for both of us.

Lesson 9: Put yourself in the other person's shoes.

CHAPTER
TEN

DEVELOP CLEAR AGREEMENTS
Why Agreements Take the Stress out of Disagreements

During a parliamentary debate in the House of Commons members aren't allowed to speak directly to one another. Instead, in order to abide by the rules, they have to go through the Speaker of the House. Rather than being able simply to tell a fellow politician that they think he is rubbish, members have to say something like, 'Mr Speaker, as far as I'm concerned, the honourable gentleman is a total incompetent.' This etiquette, which might seem rather odd and certainly requires a great deal of self-control, was put in place to avoid face-to-face confrontation and all-out acrimony. During his resignation speech in 1990, Sir Geoffrey Howe managed to deliver one of the most withering critiques of a serving prime minster while referring to her throughout as, 'My right honourable friend'.[1]

It's a tradition that enables members of parliament to express strong views while reducing levels of antagonism. However, they need constantly reminding to stick to the third-person protocol. During one debate an MP commented directly to the member proposing the motion: 'Interestingly, the government's proposal to review benefits means that if you are a woman, you should consider suffocating your husband.' The Speaker of the House immediately replied, 'It is self-evident that I am not a woman, and my wife would be extremely surprised to discover that I had a husband.'

Debates are also regulated by strict codes of conduct governing what kind of language can and can't be used. When an MP crosses the line and says something considered unacceptable, it is recorded. Entries in the logbook of unparliamentary phrases differ from one country to the next.[2] The following remark made the list after being uttered in New Zealand's parliament in 1949: 'His brains could revolve inside a peanut shell for a thousand years without touching the sides.'[3] It's the kind of humour that might get children interested in politics, but it's blacklisted in parliamentary debate – at least, in New Zealand. One of the worst insults is to refer to another member as dishonourable. References to lying are also strictly taboo.

PREDICTING RELATIONSHIP BREAKDOWNS

While they're in the House, MPs have to stick to established ground rules, but the shackles are off when it comes to people's language at home. There are no formal rules stopping us from accusing each other of being liars, cheats and losers in the heat of the moment, but there are consequences. Dan and Beth have free rein to say what they like to each other, but they'll have to accept that what they say is likely to have an impact on their relationship, particularly if what they're saying becomes hurtful.

Dr John Gottman and Dr Bob Levenson are world-leading experts on relationship analysis and the characteristics of marital stability. During a study in 1983, they discovered that in 96 per cent of cases, the way people handled the first three minutes of a conflict discussion determined how it would go for its duration. If they began the conversation in a critical manner – triggering Blamestorming, Dominatricks and Escalation – it seemed to set the tone for their relationship. What's more, with over 90 per cent accuracy Gottman and Levenson found that they could predict the longer-term success or failure of any relationship, based purely on observing the way a couple discussed an area of conflict.

Gottman and Levenson were so surprised by the initial results of their research that they thought it might be down to chance. However, time and again, their findings were reaffirmed. In situations where a relationship had broken down, they discovered that the way partners had been conducting their conversations hadn't grown or evolved while they'd been together. The relationships that failed tended to be those in which the couples they observed were interacting almost identically to the way in which they'd been interacting when they'd first been studied, four years earlier. Gottman and Levenson's research confirms, beyond all doubt, that the way we conduct our conversations determines the success of our relationships.

DIFFERENT AGREEMENTS FOR DIFFERENT CONVERSATIONS

It's easy to make a false assumption and think that having clear agreements can stifle conversation. On the contrary, agreements can actually allow conversations to flow, preventing them from becoming tangled up. I've worked with hundreds of teams all over the world. The best ones all have clear rules of engagement. These aren't imposed from on-high but are made and owned by each team member as a commitment to everyone else in the team. Having agreements enables people to know where they stand, how to challenge things they disagree with and what approach to take in order to tackle issues and problems most effectively, as they arise.

When banker Ethan is asked what he does for a living he often says, 'I'm a professional meeting attender.' People laugh but they know what he means. Many of us spend too much time in meetings, often poorly conducted, way too long and with a negative return for all the time and effort.

A typical day for Ethan might go like this:

08.30–09.30

Team meeting to start the day. Conversation is mediocre and some team members pay more attention to checking emails or sending text messages.

> *What agreement is needed? Unless there's an emergency that needs attending to, agree a ban on phones, texts and emails during meetings.*

11.00–12.00

Ethan has a meeting with 10 people to discuss their marketing plan. The conversation sprawls across a host of topics until people get frustrated. 'We seem to have gone way off the point,' someone moans after 45 minutes.

> *What agreement is needed? Always begin each meeting with a clear sense of purpose, stating your objectives and intended results. Make sure everyone who attends really needs to be there.*

12.30–13.30

Ethan gets back to his desk to find 25 fresh emails in his inbox. He spends 20 minutes reading them; 80 per cent are messages that he's been copied in on unnecessarily.

> *What agreement is needed? Establish email protocols so that people don't waste time reading messages that have been sent to cover other people's backs.*

15.00–17:00

Ethan's boss sets up a team meeting to develop a new proposal. It's meant to be a creative discussion but, all too quickly, people seem to be trampling on each other's ideas.

> *What agreement is needed? When you're looking to develop new opportunities, you must agree to listen to each other's ideas. At first sight the best ideas can seem outlandish or plain mad, but that's no reason to shoot them down. At a later stage you'll need to challenge those ideas and consider reasons why they might not work, before further resources are invested in them. But, to begin with, you need to create room to explore them.*

20.15

While putting the kids to bed, Ethan takes a call from work about an IT issue. Lara starts complaining, saying he's always working. When Ethan tells her it's an emergency, she asks him why there seems to be a new one every evening. It's a bad end to the day.

> *What agreement is needed? Discuss ways of dealing with issues around working at home and managing to protect family time. As we become more and more 'connected' through new technologies, the boundaries between home life and work are becoming increasingly blurred.*

Agreements that are appropriate to the context of a relationship, team or project need to be developed and agreed. Once established, they'll allow you to navigate your way through difficult conversational territory.

In the lead up to the 2012 Olympic Games in London, I worked with the teams building the stadiums and athletes' village. For the first time since the introduction of the modern Olympics in 1896 nobody was killed during the construction process in preparation for the games, in spite of the fact that it required 46,000 people to do 77 million hours of work.[4] Far from being down to luck, this was the product of people raising their individual concerns about safety at every level of the project. By making this an agreed ground rule, people had permission to tackle difficult conversations with each other and were expected do so. Indeed, there was little tolerance for those who didn't commit to this principle and stick to it.

Many people dread the prospect of conducting conversations within large groups, often for fear that the situation will devolve into anarchy. Establishing ground rules at a meeting's outset is essential to avoid this. For example, I'll always ask people to raise challenges and questions – albeit in a respectful way – in the meeting rather than out of earshot at the coffee machine, so that we have an opportunity to resolve them. When jointly created, ground rules provide the foundation for meaningful conversations.

HAVING AGREEMENTS AT HOME

The idea of having an agreement might sound a bit official, or even rather corporate. Despite this, agreements are even more important at home. At the time of writing, the longest-married couple in the world are Karam and Kartari Chand who tied the knot in 1925 and live in Bradford, UK. Karam says he loves Kartari so much that he wants to spend another 80 years by her side.[5] The question everyone asks is how they've managed to keep their relationship intact for so many years. One of the secrets of their success is the way they give time to one another.

'Listen to each other,' Karam explains. 'The most important thing in a relationship is to listen. People don't listen any more because they are too busy with work and TV. Listen to your loved ones' problems and concerns every day.' We all know the wisdom of Karam's advice, but it's not an easy commitment to make and then stick to. Opportunities to listen might feel as if they need to be jammed into our hectic schedules. General exhaustion, work overspill, television, the internet, social networking and family commitments can combine to squeeze the life out of time dedicated to having a proper conversation.

The Marriage Course, developed by Nicky and Sila Lee, makes a very clear recommendation. Once a week, couples should spend at least two hours together in uninterrupted time, sharing their hopes, anxieties, excitements, worries and achievements as a means of building intimacy. Ideas such as this seem blindingly obvious, yet personal experience suggests they can be absurdly difficult to practise. Life gets in the way, but our relationships are at the heart of our lives. Managing this contradiction gets even more difficult if we haven't established clear agreements with each other.

WHAT TO DO?

STEP 1:
Turn Expectations into Agreements

Ethan's productivity and sense of fulfilment at work could be radically improved if he established some simple but explicit agreements with his colleagues. Whatever the context, focus on the few that will make the biggest difference rather than developing a long list; for example, creating a genuine commitment to listen to each other during work meetings will transform their effectiveness.

Conversations can fragment without an argument having to break out. Sheer earnestness to be heard or to get a point across often leads to a total absence of listening. Whether it's because we grew up in a large family, sat in a class at school with 30 other children or have highly vocal peers at work, we learn that the world is not going to wait for us to collect our thoughts. There seems to be an unspoken understanding that we need to barge our way into conversations to ensure our voice gets heard. When you're sitting in your team meetings at work you know that the pauses between people speaking will be tight, and that you'll have to jump in quickly to get into that ever-so-tiny gap. It doesn't have to be so, and having clear agreements helps mitigate this impulse.

Ethan's team would benefit from creating agreements like these, to:

- Listen, taking others' perspectives into account
- Challenge each other openly, honestly and constructively
- In every meeting, ask what's best for the customer, internally and externally
- Make time for each other
- Resolve issues quickly – don't let them fester
- In public, always back each other up.

By making these kinds of agreements explicit, people are then able to remind each other of them, as and when they might need to. They become reference points to which you can return repeatedly.

STEP 2:
Hold Each Other to Your Agreements

Reminding each other of your agreements isn't always easy. Dan and Beth have agreed that they won't let the sun go down on an argument. They'll need to remind each other of this when they're in the Bad Place and want to be left alone to sulk. If Beth does so by Blamestorming, she might say:

> *Now I suppose you're going to sulk all evening, instead of talking things through.*

This approach won't help. It would be better if she let her emotions settle after an argument and then tried:

> *We said we'd never go to sleep on an argument. Can we talk things through, so we can get things resolved?*

If they manage to sit down together, having clear ground rules will really help their conversation. Perhaps most importantly, they need to agree that they'll listen to each other *without interruption*. Rather than making mental notes of barbed one-liners in response to what they're hearing, they need to listen from the second and third perspectives. Doing this will help loosen their attachment to their own version of the truth. It doesn't mean that Beth needs to share Dan's opinion on the situation, or vice versa. But by accepting the validity of each other's perspective, they're more likely to release themselves from a position of righteousness and create a joint way forward.

Holding each other to your values, in the good times and the bad, is the basis for a strong relationship.

Lesson 10: Agreements needn't restrict you – they can give you freedom.

CHAPTER ELEVEN

SET THE CONTEXT
How to Prevent Misunderstanding and Defensive Responses

Sailing the high seas in the 16th century in search of new lands must have felt like heading into a vast chasm of uncertainty. Unpredictable weather, enemy fleets, opportunistic pirates, sketchy maps and rudimentary navigational equipment would have made it impossible to predict a safe return. And yet, as the saying goes, you couldn't discover new lands without losing sight of your own shore, perhaps for months at a time. When the scurvy-suffering, bleary-eyed crew member looking through his telescope finally shouted, 'Land ahoy!' you'd be unsure whether you'd be welcomed with garlands of flowers, spears or muskets, and whether you'd spend the evening dancing round a casserole pot with your new friends or make the uncomfortable discovery that you were destined to be the meal in the pot.

Such a precarious state of affairs led ships to the practice of raising flags to state their nationality and intentions as they advanced toward a territory, indicating whether they were friend or foe. This system has endured through the centuries and has been written into the United Nations Convention on the Law of the Sea. Flags state where you're coming from and heading to and, you hope, herald your arrival to a welcoming reception committee.

Though not quite so perilous, conversations can sometimes feel like being on the high seas because:

- They don't tend to follow a straight line
- People don't always manage to say what they mean
- Others can't be relied on to react as we'd like or may not agree with our point of view
- People may keep their intentions under wraps

- The conversation we're having might be moving at such a pace that we don't have the luxury of long pauses to assess what someone has just said before we reply.

In the face of this, it's vital that we operate our own flag system to let people know where we're coming from and heading to. If people are not able to discern this, it's hardly surprising that they sometimes go into a defensive and survival-based mode, as a way of coping with the unexpected demands of a conversation – especially when it's particularly difficult.

The words themselves represent the content of a conversation; the context is what surrounds them. It includes the preceding and subsequent words, the tone they're spoken in, body language and the intention behind the words. Being able to grasp both content and context simultaneously enables us to apprehend meaning and navigate a conversation's direction.

SEEING PART OF THE PICTURE

If the context isn't clear it's easy for a conversation to fall into Mixed Messages. In their famous 'Fork Handles' sketch of 1976, the British comedy duo Ronnie Barker and Ronnie Corbett played on the confusion that can ensue when there's a mismatch between content and context. A tight-lipped customer (Barker) goes into the local hardware store and proceeds to befuddle an increasingly exasperated shopkeeper (Corbett) as he goes through his shopping list. The hapless shopkeeper rummages through boxes to produce four candles instead of fork handles, a plug for the bath instead of one for an electric socket and letter Ps instead of tins of peas. The customer makes no effort to clarify his motives, so the shopkeeper assumes he's being taken for a ride and storms off.

Normally we're adept at recognizing when someone means balmy rather than barmy, cereal rather than serial or elicit rather than illicit, without having to check which one they're using. Understanding a person's intentions is a bit more tricky.

Without understanding the context, this conversation between my wife and our 12-year-old son could be interpreted in different ways:

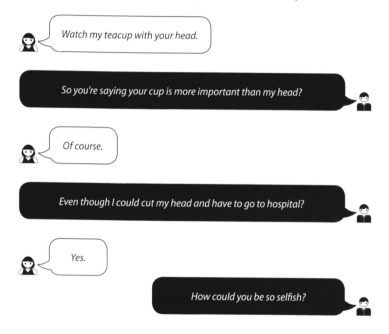

Watch my teacup with your head.

So you're saying your cup is more important than my head?

Of course.

Even though I could cut my head and have to go to hospital?

Yes.

How could you be so selfish?

They were lying in bed one Saturday morning. Marcus adopted a tone of mock outrage when Sally asked him to be careful not to knock her cup over. Both of them ended up in fits of laughter. Since both of them understood the context of the conversation, it didn't lead to Mixed Messages.

Conversations go wrong when the context isn't understood or is misconstrued. That's why sending abrasive one-liners on email without any context is a sure-fire way to irritate people. Other examples where the context leads to Mixed Messages might include: when you think you're having a playful conversation but your partner takes offence, or you're trying to be helpful but come across as interfering and dominating. While it's easier to lay the blame on someone else for getting the wrong end of the stick, we can usually do more to make our context clear.

THE ROLE OF CONTEXT

In modern English the use of the word 'context' can be traced back to the early 15th century, though its etymology reaches much further, to the Latin word *contextus*. The ancient use of the word meant 'to join together by weaving'; by implication, this involves bringing different parts together to create a whole.

With information – often in byte-sized pieces – flying at us from all directions, the world can feel increasingly fragmented. It's estimated that each day we're exposed to approximately 1,000 advertisements, from sources including TV, the internet, billboards, radio and newspapers. Over the course of a week we're exposed to a volume of information that would fill a computer's hard drive. We're overloaded with content, but it doesn't necessarily come with an accompanying context, and it's our job to make sense of it all.

While there's an immediate context for any given conversation – who's having it and why – there's also the wider context to consider. People are more motivated at work when they understand and appreciate the context in which they're doing their work: why it's important, what value it brings and the difference it will make if they strive to do it well. If they feel as if they are insignificant cogs in a large corporate wheel, they're likely to invest minimal effort and care. A study by the Corporate Leadership Council revealed that highly engaged employees were 87 per cent less likely to leave their companies than their disengaged counterparts.[1] And a study of 23,910 business units compared top-quartile and bottom-quartile engagement scores and found that those in the top quartile were on average 12 per cent more profitable.[2] This doesn't happen by accident. Great leaders spend a huge proportion of their time communicating with the people they lead to make them feel included, involved and connected to a higher purpose. I have worked with one company that ranks 'outstanding' each year in the Sunday Times 'Best Place to Work' index. The CEO dedicates a month every year to road shows with his teams across Europe. He uses this time to communicate the strategy but, more importantly, to listen. It's hardly surprising that 84 per cent of his staff said they had great faith in him as their CEO, which was one of the highest such scores in any UK company.

Those who go the extra mile in service to a cause, project or organization do so because of the context. They see opportunities for themselves and a meaningful vision for the future, and they feel that they're being fully supported in, and acknowledged for, their work.

WHERE IT GOES WRONG

In the following examples the context isn't clearly communicated, leading to unintended consequences:

[1] Mia, who's a social worker, is given some feedback by her boss. She's highly regarded at work and is seen as someone with the potential for

promotion in the coming year, but her boss assumes she knows this and starts their conversation by saying:

> *As you know, we've gathered some feedback from your colleagues and there are a few areas that have come to light that I want to discuss.*

Mia's left feeling offended as well as unsure about where she stands in relation to her long-term future as a social worker, while her boss is surprised at her reaction to his comments and by her defensive demeanour.

[2] Ravi's been working on an IT project for months. While he's busy working on it late one evening, he gets an email that's been written by the IT director, forwarded to him by a colleague:

```
Sorry. Got some issues related to the new release.
Will need to pause the project. Hopefully back on
track very soon.
```

This email comes out of the blue and Ravi only understands a fragment of the background to the decision. Without the wider context he ends up feeling totally disenfranchised. Another company has recently approached him with a job offer and he decides to talk to them.

[3] Diane is headteacher at the local primary school, and Beth's boss. She has a 15-year-old son called Ben who moans that he's constantly being nagged about his exam revision. She thinks he's not doing enough work and is worried that he's destined for academic failure. The pressure he feels to achieve academic success is heightened by the fact that his mother heads up a school. Every time the subject is mentioned, their conversation moves toward Escalation. This only makes the situation worse.

[4] Rather than writing separate replies to work emails, Diane tends to write comments alongside the messages she's received. In order for her notes to stand out, she writes short answers in RED CAPITALS such as: YES, NO, NOT SURE – NEED TO TALK. Yui, who's Japanese, is a member of Diane's teaching staff. She finds Diane's replies rude and feels as if Diane is shouting. For Diane it's simply a time-saving device.

In each case, problems arise not so much due to the content, but because the conversation's context hasn't been established to enable both parties to share a mutual understanding.

WHAT TO DO?

STEP 1:
Put Up Your Flag

The conversation between Mia and her boss would have progressed more positively if he'd given some thought to how he might have set it up – perhaps beginning like this:

> *Mia, you're highly valued and we're really keen for you to progress to a more senior role. You're already exceptionally strong in some areas and will need to develop in others.*

Mia's boss may go on to ask her where *she* thinks she's stronger and weaker, and what her ambitions are. In the process, he may also give her feedback about the areas of her work he thinks she could improve. He could still communicate this in a straightforward and direct manner – there's no need to prevaricate – but first, he should set a context in which Mia can hear what he has to say with openness and positivity.

STEP 2:
Acknowledge Concerns

You'll establish a stronger connection with someone you're talking to if you can reflect what they may be thinking or feeling.

It would make a difference to Ravi if his boss Steve said:

Ravi, I know you've worked flat-out for the last three months to get this project over the line, and I know it's frustrating and demoralizing when these things get pulled at the last minute. But I really am extremely grateful for your efforts. Look, this is the background to the decision – just so you understand what's going on …

STEP 3:
Express Commitment

Having drawn the conclusion that Diane's nagging him all the time, it becomes difficult for teenager Ben to listen with the feeling that she can really help him. Diane needs to engage Ben in a longer conversation that she should start by making her commitment to him very clear and by bringing any subtext into the open:

> *I know I sound like a constant nag. I'm not out to spoil your fun, and I'm not expecting A grades in everything either. But I do want you to have choices about what you do after leaving school. I want to be able to support you but I'm struggling to know how. Can we talk?*

STEP 4:
Seek to Understand Each Other's Context

Yui doesn't say anything to Diane about her emails, but when she's at home she complains to her boyfriend about Diane's lack of courtesy. It has a strong effect on her motivation at work.

Meanwhile, Diane is oblivious to the cultural nuances causing offence for Yui. If she was aware of the issue, she could modify her emails – or set the context by explaining why she replies as she does. What Yui doesn't realize is that Diane's terse email responses are a means of coping with a hundred messages a day, many of which she has to catch up on late at night. Their failure to understand each other's context leads to the Tangle.

Diane and Yui's example highlights our need to talk to one another about our individual style of communication. In any aspect of life, misunderstandings are inevitable. What's important, though, is to check regularly what we need to be doing more or less of – or what we should be continuing to do – in our conversations with those around us. As a consequence, the job of navigating our way through difficult conversations is made so much easier.

Lesson 11: Content always sits inside context.

CHAPTER
TWELVE

CLEAR UP THE MESS
How to Say 'Sorry' and Clear Up Disagreements

There are few words more weighted with meaning than 'sorry'. According to one survey, in the UK alone it's uttered 368 million times every day.[1] It's a word that's developed multiple meanings ranging from complete acceptance of responsibility to an exclamation we make when someone bumps into us, which roughly translates as: 'Look where you're going!'

The history of literature offers an insight into its varied meanings over time. Plato's *Apology* is his account of a speech made by Socrates in 399 BC that doesn't actually contain a sniff of an apology. Put on trial for not recognizing the gods, Socrates sets the scene by saying that his accusers 'have hardly spoken a word of truth'.[2] What follows is a withering verbal attack. Plato's title only makes sense when it's explained that ἀπολογία (or apologia) means 'defence' in Greek.

Fast-forward to 1606 and Shakespeare's Macbeth appears on stage after murdering King Duncan, with bloody dagger in hand. Macbeth has cleared his way to the crown, but instead of experiencing delight he states grimly, 'This is a sorry sight'.[3] In contrast to Socrates' confident defence, Macbeth's 'sorry' is laden with remorse, guilt, paranoia and the onset of madness.

Carry on to the present day and we see that a simple word can still convey multiple meanings:

- I'm sorry and I take full responsibility
- I'm sorry but, for the record, I was right
- I'm sorry, but you had it coming
- I'm sorry, but I was an innocent victim of circumstances
- I'm sorry, but you did over-react

- I'm sorry, but I can't remember a thing and therefore can't be responsible
- I'm sorry, but you provoked me and therefore it's technically your fault
- I'm sorry if I'm wrong, but I doubt it
- I'm sorry. Now where's your apology?
- I'm sorry you misread what I meant
- I've said sorry, so why can't you move on?
- On the advice of my PR agent, I'm sorry.

With the exception of the first, each of these is likely to spark another row, conforming to Oscar Wilde's advice: 'Always forgive your enemies – nothing annoys them so much.'

A genuine 'sorry' – in the sense of taking responsibility without justification – is extremely powerful because there's no inference of blame or defence, and no hidden agenda. It's simply 'sorry'. It doesn't guarantee that the apology will be accepted, or that any hurt caused is resolved, but it's a clear acknowledgement of my role in something that didn't work for you.

THE MESSY NATURE OF CONVERSATION

Clearing up the mess doesn't always have to involve offering an apology, but it does demand thinking about what will settle, heal or even enhance a situation or relationship. Without making any excuses for poor conduct, we have to accept that conversation can be a chaotic business and doesn't unfold in straight lines. It can be bewildering, fast moving, messy, exhilarating and infuriating in equal measure. As such, it would be ridiculous to imagine that you're going to get all your conversations right.

It's worth noting that people have different ways of dealing with conflict. Some people report high levels of fulfilment in their personal relationship while rarely tackling disagreements head-on. They've developed ways of simply 'getting over it' when they clash with their partner, without having to delve into the details once they've both cooled down. There's a sound principle behind this. Making space and creating distance allows time to take the second and third perspectives; enabling both parties to get down from their high horse and move on without a residue of ill feeling.

However, it's unrealistic to expect to go through life without having to address a difficult conversation from time to time. Whether we've been in the Tangle, the Big Argument, the Bad Place or the Lock Down, there are occasions when we need to revisit a situation, if only to untangle crossed wires, repair emotional damage or work out how to avoid a Groundhog Day-type situation in which the same kind of disagreement is repeated again and again.

How can we increase the odds of a constructive outcome?

THE LOCK DOWN

It's worth focusing on the Lock Down, as this can be the toughest situation to address. Imagine someone metaphorically pulling down the portcullis on any further communication and putting up a large 'No Entry' sign. The person is hurt or angry, or both, and doesn't want to talk. Sometimes there can be a case for allowing time and space for a natural healing process to take place, rather than trying to force the issue and creating even more acrimony. Equally, having the tools to address this kind of situation would give you choice and the potential to resolve things more rapidly.

Headteacher Diane has a flare-up with her 17-year old-daughter Abby, who demonstrates zero tact when she suddenly comes out with, 'Can you pick me up at 11pm from the party on Thursday?' Abby's timing is impeccably bad: Diane's had a shocking day at work and has just pulled a burned pizza out of the oven. To make matters worse, she has no recollection of a party on Thursday and the idea of an 11pm pick-up on a school evening is inconceivable when Abby is meant to be revising for her exams. She's riled by her daughter's expectant tone and doesn't help matters by twice referring to Abby as 'young lady', in a way that emphasizes her own rank. The conversation concludes with slammed doors, Abby in the Lock Down in her bedroom and an untouched meal going cold on the kitchen table.

In retrospect, Diane could have avoided an argument if she'd deferred it. Getting the timing right is vital. She could have put off confronting Abby until a better moment and given herself more thinking time in the process:

Can you pick me up at 11pm from the party on Thursday?

Let's talk a little later when I can concentrate on what you're asking.

But I said I'd let Hannah know.

Well, I'm sorry. Hannah will have to wait.

Can I just tell her 'yes'?

Please, Abby, let's talk a bit later. I'm tired and rather busy right now. You'll get a much better response if you give me an hour.

However, now that the damage is done, Diane is aware that the impasse with Abby could rumble on for a few days. She decides to tackle the situation immediately rather than letting it fester. This isn't easy, since the golden rule when tackling the Lock Down is to allow time for an abundance of listening and Diane doesn't actually feel as if she's done anything wrong. The following exchange is likely to make matters worse:

(Diane peers around the bedroom door.)

Abby, I'm sorry I barked at you.

(Abby stares at her phone.)

Abby, please … can we talk?

 I don't want to discuss it. I can't believe you said no …

Abby, come on. It's hardly fair to put all the blame on me!

With her last comment Diane has dropped into Abby's mode and the row will spark off again. This time it could get even worse. It's vital that Diane isn't drawn into Blamestorming. She's going to have to park her side of the story for a while and listen.

GETTING BACK IN COMMUNICATION

To get the conversation going, Diane needs to recognize Abby's feelings and ask open questions without rising to Abby's barbed comments. She also needs to consider Abby's viewpoint by adopting the second perspective:

> *I know you feel very upset and aggrieved about this.*
> *Can you tell me what the plan was for Thursday?*

> *I told you about two weeks ago. You never remember anything.*
> *Hannah's having a birthday party ... Duuuhhh!*

> *OK. I don't remember. Can you tell me again?*

> *You do remember. I said we were having drinks at hers and a meal out.*
> *There's only six of us and it has to be a Thursday because Hannah's busy*
> *that weekend and going on holiday as soon as term finishes.*

> *OK. Let me just check what you're saying …*

If Diane can stick with the conversation and ask questions without making Abby feel wrong, there'll be a point where there's enough space for her to express her own feelings. When she does, she'll be better off naming the issues that were in the subtext of their flare-up earlier. These have more to do with underlying feelings than with the timing of the party itself.

> *I'm worried that you've got exams coming up and that you might run out of time and mess them up. I'm also quite stressed and tired and really don't relish the idea of coming out at 11 o'clock to pick you up. We did make a deal that you wouldn't go out in the week during term time but I don't want to spoil your fun and I know you need a break now and again.*

If Diane can express her subtext without dropping into Blamestorming, it would open the door for Abby to express her subtext too:

> *Mum, if you come any earlier I'll be totally humiliated. Everyone would be going on about how I was tucked up in bed while they were still at the party. I know you've got a lot on at the moment, but I promise I won't be late. I can see if Hannah's mum will drop me home.*

As their affinity gets restored, they quite naturally move into negotiation and, with a new-found willingness to compromise, reach a mutually acceptable solution. To get it to this point, Diane has had to bite her lip and let Abby have her say, at least during the conversation's early stages. By keeping her equanimity and detaching from her instinct to react, Diane has created the space for communication. The heaviness of the conversation begins to lift and some humour – though ironic at first – creeps back in.

This hasn't meant Diane's become a doormat. It could be that she may have to insist on saying 'no', but it's vital she listens to Abby first and explains the context of her response rather than ending up being dragged into a brawl and pulling rank. Once they reach an amicable solution, Diane may want to set some ground rules in relation to Abby's attitude and timing. This will have to come toward the end of the conversation. If Diane started to lay down the law at this point it would feel to Abby as if she was being lectured and she would probably turn off.

WHAT TO DO?

The principles of listening and of taking an alternative perspective are applicable both when seeking to prevent a conversation from going wrong and when trying to get out of a messy conversational situation. There are several practices to keep in mind.

STEP 1:
Apologize Without Justification

It's probably better not to apologize at all if you're going to follow it up by attempting to justify yourself or blame someone else. Apology and blame are like oil and water. If you're going to say sorry, do it without any sense of self-righteousness or inference that you deserve a sainthood for doing so. There's nothing that will rile other people more.

STEP 2:
Ask Open Questions and Hear Them Out

If someone's in the Lock Down you need to ask open questions that invite them to express their feelings and point of view. Again, don't venture into this territory unless you're willing to listen to what they have to say, even if you think it's untrue or unjustified. Your job is to hear them out fully, even to reflect on what they're saying, letting them know you're listening by mirroring this back to them – challenging though this might be:

So you're saying you think it's unfair of me to expect you to …

I make no promises that it's an easy process, but demonstrating that you can listen, and hear what's being said without interrupting, can help someone move out of the Lock Down.

STEP 3:
Put Your Own Story on Hold

If you're going to truly listen to someone else's perspective, you have to be able to put your story on hold until you've heard theirs. While you do this, your job isn't to prepare your own defence – unless, of course, you're in a court of law, in which case the rules are entirely different and a judge will determine the outcome.

When you do get an opportunity to speak, it's worth acknowledging that you're recounting your story as opposed to the truth of the matter – even though you may feel that the two are the same thing. If you can accept that the other person has a legitimate version of events, you can listen so that you understand it rather than constructing evidence in your mind about why they are wrong.

STEP 4:
Get Back to What's Important

Whenever I work with people who are locked in a disagreement, I'm amazed at how often the chasm between those involved doesn't look nearly as wide – or can even disappear altogether – once they're in open communication with each other. They often see that they have the same commitments and values even though they have different styles of expression or views about how to deliver on these commitments. Once they've listened to one other they naturally start to look for ways forward. However, the process has to start with listening.

While conflict can be healthy, it's important to remember that there are two types – one is proactive and productive, the other is bitter and toxic. To keep a conversation healthy, you have to be able to navigate your way through differences of opinion without running into treacherous currents, or you need the tools to repair the damage if the conversation goes awry. As long as you've genuinely accepted your part in the problem, saying 'sorry' is a good start.

Lesson 12: Say 'sorry' without giving your story.

CHAPTER
THIRTEEN

WATCH YOUR LANGUAGE – AND OTHER PEOPLE'S
What You Can Learn from the Way People Talk

People often think that you need to pay close attention to someone's body language in order to tell if they are lying. Not so, according to UK-based psychologist Professor Richard Wiseman, who conducted a national survey about lying. As part of the research he interviewed the veteran TV presenter Sir Robin Day on the BBC science programme *Tomorrow's World*, questioning him about *Gone with the Wind* and *Some Like It Hot*. The idea was that Sir Robin would describe in turn why each film was his all-time favourite. In reality, he loved one of the films and found the other to be a terrible bore.

Having answered the same five questions about each film, the public were asked to vote and 30,000 people responded. Of these, 52 per cent were right to think he'd lied about *Gone with the Wind* and 48 per cent thought he'd lied about *Some Like It Hot*. The right answer was fairly irrelevant; the split vote proved the point that people struggled to tell which was which.

Wiseman's conclusions, published in his book *Quirkology*, are in line with the findings of other experts in the field: there's no reliable differentiation in body language between liars and truth-tellers; the difference is in the language.[1] When lying, Sir Robin's responses were nearly half the length of his responses when he was being truthful. He also made fewer references to his feelings, suggesting that when people lie they try to give away as little as possible. Moreover, he only used the word 'I' twice while talking about *Gone with the Wind*, compared to seven times for *Some Like It Hot*.

LEAVING A TRAIL OF CLUES

Our language provides an insight into our past. For example, the average work meeting contains terminology that reflects our bloody heritage. We talk about being *held to ransom* or *going in for the kill* when closing a deal. Companies are *ambushed* and *crushed* by the competition and *vie for supremacy* in their markets. We are *bombarded* with emails, *battle* through our to-do lists and complain that our ideas were *torpedoed*. People discuss whether it's safe to *stick a head above the parapet*, and the ultimate sanction is to be *fired*.

Such expressions are like a plane's vapour trails, leaving evidence of what's gone before. These days it's not so much our physical survival that's at stake, but the survival of our identity and our reputation – who we consider ourselves to be. Some people even have a bizarre way of talking about their 'personal brand', as if they're a product dreamt up in a marketing workshop.

A person's choice of words can also tell you a lot about what she is thinking and feeling. A doctor reported that he received the notes on a new patient, and the previous doctor's last entry was: 'Pain in neck. Has. Is.'[2] It's not hard to work out what was going through the doctor's mind.

Language also provides intelligence about the way someone processes information. If a person tends to say, 'I need to think about this,' it probably indicates that they're quite reflective by nature. They usually prefer to have space to mull over their options rather than feel that they're being pushed into making rapid decisions. In contrast, people who are more oriented toward their feelings will talk about following their instincts. If something feels right, they will tend to go with it.

The ability to decode linguistic cues is an incredibly useful tool that has relevance in every walk of life. I find it invaluable with my children – one of whom tends to be reflective while the other two are extroverts. It works best for my reflective daughter if I drop an idea into a conversation and then come back to it at a later point, allowing her time to consider things. This avoids arguments that would probably flare up if she felt she was being pushed toward something. Understanding the way she processes information – and becomes clear about what she thinks – enables me to communicate with her in a style that's more accessible to her, rather than expecting her to conform to my own preferred style of communication.

For my other two children, their method of processing tends to be the conversation itself. I'm better off asking them how they *feel* about a situation than what they *think*. Bear in mind, though, that people who are feelings-oriented may benefit from thinking things through a little more before jumping to a decision. Some well-chosen questions often won't go amiss.

The same principle applies at work. If someone's reflective, it would be a good idea to approach them after a meeting to ask them if they have any further thoughts. Chances are, they'll have done a stack of mental processing and will have something to say that's well worth listening to. If eyes are the window to the soul, language is definitely the window to the mind. Paying attention to how someone uses it can help facilitate more effective communication.

SPEAKING THEIR LANGUAGE

Ethan is a great example of someone who makes logical decisions and doesn't want ideas suddenly sprung on him. He needs time to consider an idea, weigh up the options, gather evidence and then come to a conclusion. In contrast, this isn't Lara's style at all. She makes the mistake of using her personal style when introducing an idea. It pushes Ethan into Yes, But … mode.

> *When we get the kitchen done, I'd like to get an architect to draw up plans for adding an extension on top – to use for another bathroom.*

> *Woah … hang on a minute. Where did that come from?*

> *There's no need to 'Woah' about it. It'll add stacks of value to the house and it'll be really useful when we've got guests.*

> *Sure, and it'll also cost a fortune and we'll never recover the money. I don't see the point in paying an architect to draw up plans for something we're not going to do.*

When Lara says: 'I want to get an architect', Ethan hears: 'I've decided to get an architect'. This gets them off to a bad start. He reacts to the fact that she doesn't seem to be taking a methodical approach. Meanwhile, his Yes, But … response makes Lara feel he's being dismissive and defensive. 'After all,' she says to herself, 'it's only an idea and he hasn't given it *any* consideration.' But Ethan's been caught unprepared. He doesn't see the point in encouraging an idea that he feels hasn't been thought through. The conversation moves into Blamestorming and Escalation:

The problem is – whenever I have an idea, you manage to squash it with your big 'Finance Director' shoes.

That's not true. It would help if you thought your ideas through first.

What? Have I got the intelligence of an amoeba?

It's got nothing to do with intelligence. If you're going to employ an architect, you …

Yeah, yeah … you need to think it through. In case you forgot, I'm not one of your minions at work …

It would have helped if Lara had initiated the conversation in a different way. Here's how she might have started:

Do you think we could have a chat about an idea I've had for the house, sometime?

Oh, what's that?

It doesn't have to be now, but sometime would be good.

No, now's fine.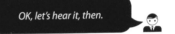

Now Lara has Ethan's attention she may want to set the context so that he knows how to listen. This will avoid the conversation going off the rails.

Please remember this is only an idea. I'm not about to make a sudden decision or rush into anything.

OK, let's hear it, then.

Lara's thought about how to broach the subject in Ethan's style. She takes a methodical approach:

You know what a pain it is when we have anyone to stay, with only the one toilet and bathroom upstairs?

Yeah …

I noticed Number 7's on the market again. They put in a kitchen, like we're going to do, but they also built an extension upstairs for a second bathroom. The house has gone on sale for £100,000 more than they paid for it. It got me thinking – since the layout of their house is identical to ours.

Oh … so your plan is to do the same thing?

Well, the builders have got to make a flat roof for the new kitchen and since they're here anyway … I just thought it might be worth exploring.

This is a much better start. Lara's introduced her idea in a logical and systematic way. She knows Ethan's going to need to mull it over so she doesn't push him. She's taking it one step at a time.

EXPECT CONCERNS AND LISTEN TO THEM

When a new idea is introduced, Ethan's concerns will always rise to the surface. It's simply his method of mental processing, and Lara needs to listen:

It's all very well to say it's selling for £100,000 more, but how much of that is down to the extension? House prices have gone up anyway.

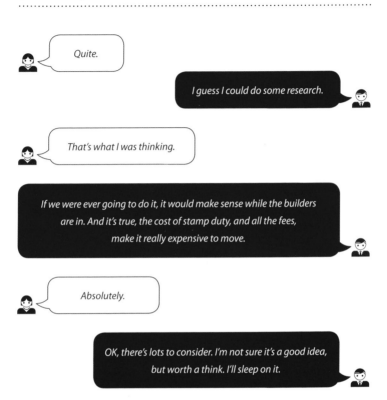

Quite.

I guess I could do some research.

That's what I was thinking.

If we were ever going to do it, it would make sense while the builders are in. And it's true, the cost of stamp duty, and all the fees, make it really expensive to move.

Absolutely.

OK, there's lots to consider. I'm not sure it's a good idea, but worth a think. I'll sleep on it.

Lara's done the perfect job. The best thing she could do was seed the idea. She's got Ethan thinking and she notices him researching data on house prices the following day.

Just as Lara has adapted her communication style to fit Ethan's, he could benefit from being more open-minded in response to her ideas rather than being quick to grill her underlying logic. This would allow her to feel more equal and valued in their relationship. He could do this by saying, 'Tell me more', rather than raising questions and concerns, and then listening more attentively to what she has to say. After all, her initial feelings may be right.

Ethan and Lara's processing styles are not gender-exclusive. They reflect Ethan's preference for logic-based decisions and Lara's preference for feeling-based ones. I've seen this dynamic reversed in numerous couples. Once you've grasped the way a partner, colleague or child processes information, you can adapt the way you communicate with them to get a better chance of being heard.

WHAT TO DO?

STEP 1:
Pay Attention to Language

The language people use gives you an insight into subtexts beneath the content of what they're saying.

- If people are tight lipped and formal, it's a clue that something's in the way of them openly expressing their thoughts and feelings.
- If they complain bitterly, it tells you that they're probably feeling angry or let down.
- If they use words such as 'think' or 'feel' a lot, it tells you how they process information and come to decisions. In the same way that you'd tune a radio to find the station you are looking for, you can adapt your speaking and listening so that you are on the same frequency as other people, increasing the chances of connecting with them.

STEP 2:
Mirroring Their Language

Numerous studies have shown the effectiveness of mirroring other people's language, pace of speech, volume and body language. As a broad guide, it's worth paying attention to whether someone is speaking in a visual, aural or kinaesthetic manner.

A visual person tends to say things such as 'I can't see the point,' the aural person will say, 'That doesn't *sound* right to me,' and the kinaesthetic one will say, 'That doesn't *feel* right.' People don't usually conform to one mode exclusively, but most of us have a preference in terms of how we speak and process information. Understanding these characteristics is crucial for any teacher who wants to accelerate the learning of their students; it's also invaluable in customer service and sales environments. When you mirror someone's language, it's easier for them to connect with what you're saying, and when people are totally in tune during a conversation, they'll spontaneously mirror each other's body position, tone of speech and language.

Lesson 13: Language provides clues to people's ways of thinking.

CHAPTER
FOURTEEN

ASK WHAT'S MISSING AND NEEDED
How to Avoid Getting into Blame

There's an ancient tale about two monks who were walking along a muddy road in the rain and found their way blocked by a small and fast-flowing stream. Unable to ford the torrent, a beautiful girl was standing at its edge, looking despairingly at the road beyond.

'Let me help you,' the older monk said without hesitation. Lifting the girl in his arms, he carried her over the stream.

The younger monk spent the rest of the day in silent contemplation, but when night came he couldn't contain himself any longer. 'What you did was wrong,' he said quietly. 'You know we aren't allowed contact with women. Why did you carry that girl across the stream?'

'I left the girl on the road,' the first monk said. 'Are you still carrying her?'[1]

The story offers a lesson about the way we might approach our conversations. When the monks reached the stream and saw the girl standing helplessly beside it, the older monk looked from the perspective of what was needed to help her across, while the other looked from the perspective of what he considered right and wrong.

CRITICS AS DESIGNERS

For many years I worked with Mike Harris, one of the UK's leading entrepreneurs. Mike holds the distinction of having developed, launched and led three multibillion-pound brands. As a through-and-through entrepreneur, he's hardened to the fact that any revolutionary idea will be met with howls of derision from the watching world, along with all the reasons why it's doomed to failure.

'Why would anyone do banking over the phone?' cried the commentators in the late 1980s, when there was a bank on practically every street corner. Undeterred, Mike launched First Direct, the world's first major telephone bank. It's still winning awards, over 25 years later. Then he became chairman of a new mobile phone operator called One-2-One; declaring that 20 million people in the UK would eventually own a mobile phone. The critics laughed, but One-2-One was later sold to T-Mobile for $10 billion, and there are now over 75 million mobile phones in use in the UK. Mike went on to announce the arrival of the world's first internet bank, leading the revolution in the online provision of financial services.

Understanding that people are inclined to offer negative judgments, Mike has learned to use this to his advantage by refining a theory he calls 'critics as designers'. Once he's developed an idea for a new proposition, he actively seeks out and listens to critics who'll tell him why it will never work. Armed with a list of their objections, he starts to investigate what's needed to address each of them successfully. For example:

Objection: Your telephone banking idea will never work because people hate being left on hold.
What's needed: Find a way to answer every call within three rings.

Objection: I can't stand it when I'm asked security questions on the phone, passed to a new adviser and then have to give my information again.
What's needed: When we pass on a caller, find a way to pass on their customer information, too.

Mike found that if people focus on thinking about what's *needed*, rather than wasting energy on Blamestorming, it has a dramatic effect on their levels of motivation and productivity. When applied across an entire organization, this approach releases an explosion of energy and commitment.

In a similar vein, Steve Jobs, the CEO of Apple, was constantly asked how he managed to systematize innovation at Apple, presumably so that other people could copy his approach.[2] His reply focused on the way people conduct conversations. According to Jobs, the spark for brilliant ideas is more likely to come from impromptu corridor chats, late-night phone calls and ad hoc meetings than from formal processes or neat-and-tidy procedures. He recognized that innovation is an emergent and often chaotic phenomenon that requires people to have radical ideas that can be collectively nurtured and developed through conversation. And he knew that if he could paint a compelling picture of the future and challenge people to think about what was missing or needed to get there, he'd stand the greatest likelihood of success.

THE FOUNDATION OF LEADERSHIP

The world hushed for a moment on 11 February 1990 to hear Nelson Mandela speak.[3] He had just been released from prison after 27 years – 19 years of which were spent in solitary confinement. Would he use his freedom to set a tone of Blamestorming and exact revenge on his oppressors, or offer his hand in reconciliation?

Just as Gandhi had done in August 1942 when he gave his 'Quit India' speech, Mandela held the future of a nation in his hands and resisted the temptation to opt for self-righteousness. He began by thanking the people across the world who had campaigned for his release and declared himself a humble servant who was placing 'the remaining years of my life in your hands'.

From then on, Mandela's speech was given over to explaining what he felt was *needed*. This included:

- The need to unite the people of South Africa in a single vision of the future
- The need for the State of Emergency to be ended immediately and all political prisoners to be freed
- The need for the future of the country to be determined by a body that was democratically elected on a non-racial basis
- The need for 'our white compatriots' to join in the shaping of a new South Africa
- The need for the international community to continue the campaign to stop the apartheid regime.

A 'what's needed' conversation like this is so powerful because there's no judgment involved. Mandela closed his speech by quoting the words he'd used on 20 April 1964 during his trial, where he'd stood in the dock facing the prospect of a life sentence or execution for sabotage, and expressed what he felt was *needed*:

> *I have fought against white domination and I have fought against black domination. I have cherished the ideal of a democratic and free society in which all persons live together in harmony and with equal opportunities. It is an ideal which I hope to live for and to achieve. But if needs be, it is an ideal for which I am prepared to die.*

Another example of Mandela's legendary reluctance to engage in Blamestorming occurred in 1998 when he was called to the High Court to defend his decision to launch an inquiry into racism in South African rugby.

He was up against Louis Luyt, the president of the South African Rugby Union.[4] Their courtroom confrontation looked set to be a head-to-head collision. However, as soon as he entered the court Mandela walked over to Luyt's lawyers and shook their hands, while his representatives looked on in horror. Greeting your opponents wasn't exactly courtroom protocol.

Soon after, France's President, Jacques Chirac, arrived in South Africa and Mandela asked his assistant, Zelda La Grange, to invite Luyt's lawyers to a reception with the French head of state. It seemed an extraordinary gesture. Initially, she ignored his request until he became insistent that the invitation should be sent. Mandela had no interest in the tactics of self-righteousness. He was more concerned with what was *needed* to bring about unity in South Africa.

WHAT TO DO?

STEP 1:
Adopt 'Missing and Needed' as a Thinking Practice

IT manager Ravi – who is husband to Mia and father to Yash, Ria and Jay – decides that for a complete day he's going to practise asking himself what's needed and write notes on it. This is what he wrote:

07.45

Yash comes into the kitchen in a foul mood, saying he'd get a better breakfast in prison. It's on the tip of my tongue to tell him to stop being an ungrateful brat. I think about what's needed and decide to talk to him tonight on the way back from football. I avoid a blow-up that would wreck the day and I mull on it on my way to work.

10.30

Steve [Ravi's manager] asks me whether I'm getting what I need from him. I'd prefer to avoid a difficult conversation and say everything's going fine, but when I ask myself what's needed, I decide to be honest. I say I'm concerned that he's operating at too low a level and I need more room to grow and develop. Tough conversation, but he says he's had the same feedback from someone else and promises to get better at letting go.

14.30

Chris [Ravi's colleague] tells me there's a problem with the delivery date on the new middleware release, and he complains that the sales team keep changing the parameters. Normally I'd jump straight in with advice, but instead ask him what he thinks is needed. It stops him in his tracks. After a bit of thought he says he needs to organize a meeting with all the parties to review the launch assumptions – a good way forward.

17.30

I ring to check why Mia's birthday present hasn't arrived. I paid so it would arrive in three working days but nothing's been delivered and Mia's birthday is the day after tomorrow. I'm given a lame excuse that it's been dispatched from the warehouse and is out of their hands. I come close to shouting when I'm referred to the small print on the website, but I think about what's needed and ask to speak to a supervisor. When I get passed on, I explain in a level way that I feel misinformed and let down. The representative calls the delivery company while I'm on the phone and confirms they'll deliver tomorrow as long as someone's in to receive it. The supervisor says she'll refund the cost of the postage.

19.45

Bringing Yash back from football, I say he seemed grumpy this morning and ask him if he's OK. He says that yesterday he had a row with a friend on the way back from school and that they sorted it out today. He says sorry for being a pain this morning. I think about what's needed in this situation and drop what I'd planned to say. No need for any lectures. He seems to have got the point.

As you go through your day, keep asking what's needed. The question will reliably lead to a different and more productive answer than the one that's produced by asking yourself who's right or wrong – or what your opinion is. If you could establish this as an ongoing practice in a work team it would revolutionize the quality of your meetings, but it's no less potent in a family or community setting.

By asking what's missing and what's needed in each situation, you remove the drama and stress of Blamestorming, allowing for more rewarding and constructive conversations.

STEP 2:
Look from a Perspective of What's Important to You

When you ask what's missing and needed, it's vital to be clear what your reference point is. Bill, Daniel and Beth's next-door-neighbour, is well meaning but very quick to lean his elbow on the gatepost and offer the benefit of his advice. This can range from a broad-brushed commentary on the political landscape to a mini-lecture on how Daniel and Beth can improve their garden. Tact isn't his strength.

Here's an example where Bill catches Daniel:

Hello, Daniel, are you all right?

Yes, thanks, Bill. How about you?

Yes, I'm bearing up. You've got a lot of weeds coming through your front lawn.

Oh, er … well, I suppose we've got a few. We haven't got around to tackling them yet – been a bit busy.

You know how you to get rid of them, don't you?

How's that? Weed killer?

Well, Daniel, you need to tackle them early, before they get deep roots and start to spread. It's important to get a spring feed for your lawn, which will kill the weeds and nourish the grass. I've got a friend who's a green keeper at the golf club and he's got a rule of thumb that he always sticks to …

Bill's sentences come in a continuous stream, without gaps between them; Dan grits his teeth. He doesn't like being called Daniel, and neither does he appreciate being given advice that he hasn't asked for. The situation is a difficult one, since Dan and Beth can choose their friends but not their neighbours. And when Dan complained to Bill that his cat was leaving its mess in the front garden, Bill appeared to take great offence and ignored them for a month.

If you asked Dan for his opinions, he'd say that Bill is rude and obsessively interfering – and at times Dan would like nothing more than to tell Bill so. However, if Dan looks from the perspective of what's important to him, it's to treat people with respect and to have good neighbourly relations. In light of this, he concludes that trust and relationship are missing and that what's needed is a different strategy for dealing with Bill. This includes the following:

- Dan needs to remember to look from the second perspective. When he does, he realizes that Bill:
  - isn't badly intended or meaning to be insulting
  - can't see the importance of setting the context when he starts a conversation
  - doesn't realize that advice isn't welcome unless it's asked for.

When he remembers this, Dan doesn't take Bill's comments so personally.

- He decides he's not going to have a full-blown conversation with Bill about his manners – this doesn't seem appropriate or necessary.
- Dan can ask Bill to stop calling him Daniel. He can do this without being confrontational, telling him it reminds him of his grandparents, who

insisted on using the full name on his birth certificate and railed against the modern tendency to shorten everything.

- If, from time to time, he needs to have a difficult chat with Bill, he'll make sure he sets the context for it. By flagging where he's coming from, it's likely that Bill will be less prickly.
- Dan decides that every so often he'll have a catch-up with Bill to maintain good relations, but that he'll need to cut the conversation short at other times. He can do this politely, saying that he's got a deadline, which is usually true.

Dan's decisions help remove negative feelings from the situation and give him a sense of control and responsibility; he no longer feels that he's the victim of Bill's behaviour. By returning to his values, and thinking about what's missing and needed for him to act in relation to them, he has a way forward that's more satisfying and has more integrity than avoiding Bill and complaining to Beth.

Lesson 14: Don't say what's wrong – ask what's needed.

CHAPTER
FIFTEEN

STRIVE FOR CLARITY
Why Checking for Understanding Will Save You Time, Effort and Money

Back in the 1980s, Grigory Romanov, the mayor of Leningrad – now St Petersburg – was tipped to succeed Leonid Brezhnev as the new Soviet leader. He eventually lost out to Mikhail Gorbachov. Whether or not this had anything to do with a story that ran through the higher echelons of Russian society, involving his daughter's wedding, I'm not sure. It was alleged that, as mayor, Romanov had persuaded the director of the city's Hermitage Museum to lend him Catherine the Great's dinner set for the wedding reception, held in the 18th-century Tauride Palace. The story went that he was allowed to borrow it on condition he guard it with his life. Late in the festivities, a guest got to his feet and accidentally dropped a cup. Taking this as a cue for the traditional Russian gesture of good luck, the guests stood up en masse and flung the entire service into the fireplace.[1]

Muddled information or political conspiracy? Romanov denied it ever happened but, like all good stories, it stuck.

THE COST OF CONFUSION

In July 2000, the London *Observer* printed this notice:

> *In the Review section's special summer reading issue of 2 July we wrongly ascribed a reading list to Roddy Doyle, the celebrated Irish author. Unfortunately, owing to a misunderstanding, the 'Roddy Doyle' we spoke to, and who gave us a very interesting selection of summer reading, was a computer engineer from north London.*[2]

This mix-up didn't cause any long-term harm, but try this: in a study of 400 companies, employee-assessment firm Cognisco estimated that misunderstandings between workers and managers cost firms $37 billion a year.[3] On average, businesses with 100,000 employees were losing a staggering $62 million a year through misunderstandings, at an average cost of $624 per employee. This figure excluded reputational costs, such as reduced customer satisfaction and the impact on brand value.

Sometimes, misunderstandings have devastating consequences for human life. After the collision between the pleasure boat *Marchioness* and the dredger *Bowbelle* on the River Thames in 1989, the formal investigation concluded that, 'Clear instructions were not given to the forward lookout on *Bowbelle*.'[4] A truly simple action could have saved 51 lives.

Similarly, the inquiry into the death of 193 people on the *Herald of Free Enterprise* ferry in 1987 found that the inner and outer bow doors had been left open. It was assumed that the assistant bosun had closed the doors when in fact he was sleeping in his cabin and didn't hear the 'Harbour Stations' call that should have summoned him to his post.[5] The tragedy would have been avoided if the person who was meant to close the doors had to confirm that he was at his post and had indeed closed them. In the vast majority of cases, disasters are due to failures in communication rather than faulty engineering.

Most of us aren't in roles where there's so much at stake, but we still rely on conversation to get things done. Organizations, communities and families are all built on the principle of interdependence, meaning that we need to coordinate our actions with others. If we don't communicate clearly, or if we're steering off different assumptions, the process breaks down.

REDUCE MARGINS FOR ERROR

While life would be much simpler if we stuck to the principle of saying what we mean, at times we purposely obfuscate the message. If you want to make a romantic advance, playing a game of innuendo means you're less vulnerable to rejection, allowing you to evaluate the response and decide whether it's safe to make a more direct approach. Politicians create confusion by deploying the art of 'substitution' during interviews, by which they answer the questions they *wish* they'd been asked rather than the ones they were *actually* asked. This strategy is not confined to the political battlefield, since children use it to great effect with their parents and teachers, and it comes in handy at work, too. It's hardly surprising that we can be left scratching our heads or that the dynamics of conversation can feel frighteningly hard to fathom.

At other times an idea seems perfectly clear conceptually, but comes out like a ball of knotted string when we try to express it. Mitt Romney was the subject of extensive press coverage for the following quote, attributed to him while he fought for the US presidency in the 2012 elections:

> *I believe in an America where millions of Americans believe in an America that's the America millions of Americans believe in. That's the America I love.*[6]

While we may not sound as convoluted as Romney, being able to communicate with crystal clarity is a real challenge for all of us. On top of this, it's never guaranteed that the people you are speaking to are listening anyway. How often have you been in a meeting in which someone's asked for a recap, and then heard a variety of versions of what was actually said?

The solution for most everyday situations is to check your own understanding and ask people to confirm theirs.

For example, a recipe for confusion occurs while Diane's pulling together the information pack for the quarterly governors' board meeting at the primary school she heads up:

> Beth, could you produce a report for the month-end governors' meeting?

> Yes, that should be fine.

By changing the conversation slightly, Beth can reduce the likelihood of the Tangle ensuing. It might add 30 seconds to their exchange but would circumvent any potential areas of confusion and save the hours of lost time that might otherwise result:

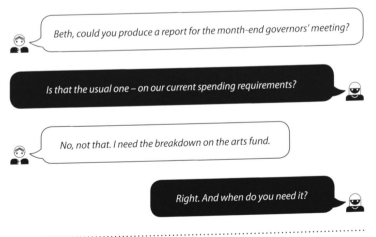

> Beth, could you produce a report for the month-end governors' meeting?

> Is that the usual one – on our current spending requirements?

> No, not that. I need the breakdown on the arts fund.

> Right. And when do you need it?

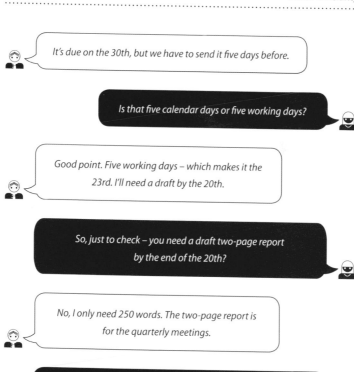

It's due on the 30th, but we have to send it five days before.

Is that five calendar days or five working days?

Good point. Five working days – which makes it the 23rd. I'll need a draft by the 20th.

So, just to check – you need a draft two-page report by the end of the 20th?

No, I only need 250 words. The two-page report is for the quarterly meetings.

Ah, right, now I'm clear. In that case, I'll do it by 5pm on Friday.

Beth is pushing for clarity – just as well too, because she could have wasted time on a long report that wasn't necessary.

CLARIFY SPECIFIC ACTIONS

Beth's conversation with Diane raises a point about clarifying action. Some exchanges are only intended to establish information and context, with no specific follow-through expected. Others need to be formulated as a specific request if you want anything to happen. A note was sent out to the parents at my children's school asking them to generate support for an open day. It read like this:

> *We hope you don't mind us asking you for help, but wondered if it wasn't too much of an imposition if you might be kind enough to please forward this invitation on – possibly to friends, neighbours or work colleagues. It would be most appreciated, but of course you are under no obligation at all to do so. With many thanks in advance for your kind assistance and kindest regards ...*

It's not hard to decipher the subtext, which reveals an underlying concern about imposing. Unfortunately, it's unlikely to have an effect. Without a clear request, you may as well sit on your hands and do nothing.

The same principle applies at work. I've sat in leadership meetings with companies that have tens of thousands of employees, and I have been aghast at the lack of rigour when it comes to conversations that need to produce action.

Ethan gets copied into the following email regarding an internal meeting at his bank:

```
Louis: Tuesday 12:44
Hi all. I would really like to get some time together
next week if possible. Which days would be good or if
next week is not doable what other dates do you have?
```

Matt: Tuesday 13:45
I've already got three hours blocked out on Monday
morning from 9am, which I thought was for a follow-up
to last week's meeting?

Louis: Wednesday 12:53
Sorry, the Monday meeting is changing from a meeting
to a conference call and will not need attendance from
you guys. That said, I think it's still important that
we get together. So, can we still get a couple of
hours next week?

Andrew: Thursday 07:53
Sorry folks. I'm struggling next week as I'm into
final prep stages, then I'm away the following week.

In the end, the meeting never happened because it wasn't signalled with
a request to do something specific by a given time. Louis may have got a
different result if he'd sent this email:

Andrew, Matt and Ethan,
To follow up from our meeting on Friday, we need two
hours together next week. By 6pm today, please would
you reply with your availability for Monday, Tuesday
or Thursday? In response, I will confirm the best day
and time by 10am tomorrow morning.

In this email Louis is being specific about what's required – two hours next Monday, Tuesday or Thursday – and he asks for a reply by a specific time – 6pm today. He also gives a commitment to get back to his colleagues by a given time tomorrow. By doing this Louis has significantly increased the odds of a meeting happening.

Due to their sheer size, larger organizations have immense potential for confusion. Company strategies tend to be based on hundreds of assumptions regarding the market, the spending power of customers, inflation, competitors and the anticipated success of future products. In addition, there are assumptions about the organizational structure and how people are developed, rewarded and disciplined. Many of these assumptions are hidden from sight for the majority of employees, meaning that the potential to get into the Tangle is huge.

WHAT TO DO?

STEP 1:
Check for Understanding while Clarifying Your Own

Even if you think you've been clear in your communication with someone else, check that they've understood you. The same principle applies in reverse. Your understanding of what someone's said to you may not match what they actually said or meant. It could prove very useful, and there's no harm in saying:

Before you go any further, let me check if I've understood …

I ask this question at regular intervals during meetings and there are often diverse opinions about what's been said. Checking for understanding, as you go along, is basic good practice when it comes to conversation.

STEP 2:
Check for Accountability and Action

However convivial, energizing or inspiring a meeting is, it won't drive things forward unless it involves clear conversations to generate and establish action. Three things need to be agreed to do this: exactly *what* will be delivered, *by whom* and *by when*. If any one of these is omitted, the chances of the action being delivered as expected are drastically reduced. Practise this approach consistently and you'll see productivity increase. It's a small change that makes a big difference.

While some conversations can be loose and broad, others need to be sharp as a knife.

Lesson 15: It costs nothing to check for clarity, but it can cost a fortune not to.

CHAPTER
SIXTEEN

REMOVE INTERRUPTIONS
How to Focus on the Conversation You're Actually Having

There's a scene in the Disney film *The Jungle Book* where the boy, Mowgli, has been taken hostage by the monkeys and handed to King Louie, the orang-utan. It's up to Bagheera, a sensible and pragmatic black panther, to explain the rescue plan to Baloo, who's a rather irrepressible bear. Predictably enough, chaos ensues when Baloo gets distracted by the groove of the music. Dancing into the fray, all he can say is, 'I'm gone, I'm *solid gone*!'

Similar exchanges happen every day as we compete for the attention of people who are 'solid gone'. The battle to avoid interruptions and to focus on what's in front of us has become tougher in an age in which we're being bombarded by stimuli. Since the internet became public in 1991, the amount of information reaching us has proliferated. Emails, texts, phone calls, instant messaging and advertising all seek to grab our attention. Managers come back from their holidays to find thousands of new emails waiting for them. It gives them a dilemma: do they face the mountain on their return or read their messages while they're away? Neither is a welcome option.

Interruptions can include physical intrusions that break our concentration and also mental interruptions, where we lose internal focus. Harvard University psychologists Matthew Killingsworth and Dan Gilbert used an iPhone application to gather data from 2,250 participants, aged 18 to 88, on subjects' thoughts, feelings and actions as they went about their daily lives. They concluded that people spend 46.9 per cent of their waking hours thinking about something other than what they're doing. What's more, their study drew a link between a wandering mind and an unhappy one.[1] The same principle applies to conversation: when we're fully present, both our conversations and our relationships are more stimulating and fulfilling.

The constant flow of information vying for our attention, much of it relatively subliminal, exposes us to more ambiguity than ever before – and this creates stress. Of course, the consequences of the information age are double-sided. The blurring of boundaries between work and home can offer remarkable opportunities in terms of flexibility and choice, but it also means that we tend to be less 'in the moment' in each environment. In turn, we begin to engage less in the tasks in front of us. We try to multitask, but there's evidence indicating that if a task requires any form of cognitive effort, multitasking means that it will take 50 per cent longer and include 50 per cent more mistakes.[2] We half-listen to others and are less attentive to the here and now. Over time we can end up feeling removed from the life we'd like to be leading.

SAWUBONA

There's a wonderful Zulu greeting that begins with someone saying 'Sawubona' – which means, 'We see you.' The response is 'Yabo sawubona' – which means, 'Yes, we see you, too.' It's an invitation to participate in each other's life and emphasizes the idea of being mentally and emotionally engaged, rather than simply being physically present.

Not every conversation needs a clear purpose and outcome. It's often all the better for being spontaneous, expansive or frivolous. Whatever its nature, though, conversation should always be founded on giving someone the gift of our attention. Failing to communicate in the spirit of sawubona allows us to do no more than skim across the surface of our relationships. In contrast, the people who give us their full attention are the ones to whom we unfailingly turn when we want to be truly heard or have important decisions to make.

Notice also how *sawubona* translates into the plural 'we' rather than 'I'. It reminds us that we exist in relationship to others. '*Umuntu ngumuntu nagabantu*' is another Zulu folk saying. It means, 'A person is a person because of other people.' It's easy to forget this spirit of interdependence and reciprocity in a world obsessed with individuality and personal identity.

Finding the time and space to give your attention fully to the person in front of you should be the first step in any process of communication. Quite apart from making the ensuing conversation more effective, it establishes rapport and tells the other person, 'We see you.' It's all about learning how to clear your mind of the mental clutter that's extraneous to the conversation you're participating in.

WHAT TO DO?

STEP 1:
Carve Out Uninterrupted Time

A few years ago, while on holiday, a businessman spent an hour or two each day on the phone to his office. His calls took place next to the swimming pool where we were sitting – making it impossible not to overhear – and it became evident that his conversations were far from urgent. He discussed all manner of day-to-day matters while brushing aside the requests of his children to play, saying to them: 'Can't you see I'm on the phone?' His elder children had become immune to his behaviour, but I could see the disappointment in the eyes of his youngest daughter. She knew exactly where she stood in the ranking for his attention. I could also picture the looks on the faces of his staff back at the office each time his number came up on their phones.

We have a family rule at home that no mobile phones are to be used at the dinner table – referred to as 'No nerding'. With rare exceptions, texts, social media and phone calls can wait. After practising this for a while, I noticed that my children started reminding each other of the nerding rule. Encouraged to test this approach during important meetings in organizations, I've experimented with asking people to put their mobile phones on a table that's out of view and to leave them there till we have a break. The table pings and buzzes with incoming messages and some people are so physically attached to their phone that they struggle to leave it out of sight. But after a while they find that the world doesn't fall apart and their meetings are more efficient and fulfilling. What's more, they experience a freedom to request each other's full attention rather than tolerating conversations conducted through a cloud of disinterest and distraction.

If, like Ethan, your work requires you to be a professional meeting attender, wherever possible try scheduling 10 minutes in between each one, allowing you to switch mentally from one to the next. One company I worked with started running meetings for 50 minutes, rather than an hour. It gave people the breathing space to finish one conversation and to prepare for the next. It also had a wider impact, reminding people to make their current conversations count, rather than chasing through them while thinking about the previous or the next one. This influences individual behaviour as well as the culture of the business.

For anyone with a busy life, uninterrupted time won't happen unless you carve it out. It's well documented that we're more effective *and* happier when we're fully absorbed in something. We'd all do well to re-learn this by watching young children focusing completely on what's in front of them, whether for a minute or an hour. It brings us back to Matthew Killingsworth and Dan Gilbert's assertion that a wandering mind is an unhappy mind.

By creating periods of uninterrupted time we become more engaged with life and with other people.

STEP 2:
Choose Your Time and Place

It's worth considering how your environment could become more conducive to good conversation. For example, 71 per cent of children in the US have a TV in their bedroom and 50 per cent have a games console.[3] It's a matter of personal choice, but it may not encourage family time together.

A friend of mine who complained that he didn't see his children in the evenings – because they were always in their rooms – decided to conduct an experiment. He reconfigured his home network so it would close down at 9pm. This was met with huge resistance, but he noticed that it had surprising benefits. Shortly after the network shut down, his teenagers got bored and came out of their rooms looking for something to do. He found that they talked about their day, their homework and their friendships and their sense of connection and affinity expanded.

As teenager Abby found when she chose the wrong moment to ask her mother, Diane, to collect her from a party, it's vital to consider the appropriate time and place for a conversation. Here are a couple of additional examples:

[1] Beth wants to broach the subject of a pay review with Diane. She's nervous about mentioning it but Dan urges her to seize the opportunity at her next one-to-one, and they prepare together. On the day, Diane's previous meeting overruns. When she finally surfaces, she apologizes to Beth and says, 'Let's still have a quick catch-up, shall we?' Beth knows that the timing isn't ideal but has worked herself up for this moment and doesn't

want to back out. As soon as she opens her mouth, she realizes it's a mistake. Diane is caught off-guard and says rather brusquely:

> *Oh … I wasn't expecting that … well … I think we should talk about it at a later date. But I can't make any promises. Times are tough, you know.*

Beth realizes that she should have rescheduled the meeting. It's a classic case of right place but wrong time.

[2] Lily, Ethan's mother, has something she wants to discuss with him. It's an important conversation for her, and she thinks she's found the opportunity when she goes with him and the grandchildren to the park. In her mind, she envisages the children playing so that she and Ethan are left to chat. As it turns out, her grandson Jack is charging wildly in all directions and granddaughter Anna is grumpy. Lily opens the conversation, but Ethan has to chase after Jack. She makes a second attempt, but this time Ethan has to deal with a disagreement over ice cream and Lily gives up the cause. The park turned out to be the wrong place. Afterwards, she's reluctant to bring up the subject again, in case it seems to Ethan as if she's pestering him, so she drops it altogether.

STEP 3:
Be Willing to Say No or Negotiate

A few years ago, my wife Sally had an unexpected phone call from a tutor regarding our young son. When the tutor said that he'd never before experienced the difficulty he was having with Marcus, Sally's fears were raised to stratospheric heights, but she was surprised by what followed.

'The problem is', he explained, 'when I give Marcus his weekly homework, he negotiates!' Apparently, he would barter to do less English and more maths, or less of both. Afterwards, we had a serious chat with him about respecting authority and taking his work seriously, but privately agreed that his natural ability to negotiate – far more advanced than either of ours – is likely to stand him in good stead and shouldn't be completely drummed out of him.

When he comes home from work, Ethan regularly says to his wife Lara that he's got nothing done that day. What he means is that he's been delivering on other people's priorities, which prevents him from progressing his own. Being able to say 'no' is as important a skill as any other in conversation. It's a requirement for staying in control of your life. If you say 'yes' to everything, you're at the beck and call of other people's demands. Just as it's easy to assume mistakenly that their own point of view is the truth, people are also inclined to think that their requirements are more pressing than anyone else's. Unless you're able to challenge, decline or negotiate the terms of an agreement before taking it on, you're likely to sink under the weight of accepted promises.

If someone interrupts you, make a conscious choice as to whether you'll put the activity you were engaged in on hold, or say you'll get back to them in five minutes – or half an hour, or later that day. Whatever your decision, the aim is to be fully in the conversation that you're in.

In spite of the relentless advance in technology, again and again I hear people lamenting the lack of time and space for old-fashioned face-to-face conversation. The instinct for this is rooted deep in our psyche and for good reason, too.

Lesson 16: Being present is more valuable than being busy.

CHAPTER
SEVENTEEN

REMEMBER TO EXPERIMENT
How Changing Your Conversations Can Revitalize Your Relationships

Defining the number of words in any language is a challenging exercise. Words go in and out of fashion and one word might have a variety of meanings. In addition, some words are considered to be obsolete while others are derivative. The *Oxford English Dictionary* contains full entries for 171,476 words that are deemed to be in current use. With the exception of people whose livelihood is tied to their vocabulary, most of us rely on a small fraction of the complete lexicon. We tend to build a limited and workable catalogue of words and then stick to it, without a great deal of curiosity or desire to extend it further.

The same principle applies when it comes to conversation – we tend to settle into a familiar groove. Whether or not it works for us is a different matter. We may repeatedly have unproductive meetings at work with the same group of people, yet the familiarity of the situation somehow dilutes the urgency to do anything radically different.

Arguments also conform to well-worn pathways, accentuated by the fact that we develop biases that prime us to listen and respond to the world in pre-set ways. Changing these habitual behaviours isn't easy. Studies of patients who've experienced coronary bypass surgery show that the ratio of people who adopt healthier day-to-day habits after surgery is only 1 in 9 – even though the benefits of a changed lifestyle are crystal clear.[1] Why is this statistic so low? The answer is that we tend to opt for what we know, in preference to what will make a difference, and live for today rather than tomorrow. The same is true with conversation, in spite of the fact that consistently poor conversations will develop into unhappy relationships.

GETTING STUCK IN A RUT

When Ethan and Dan meet up at the weekend, they have a chat about work:

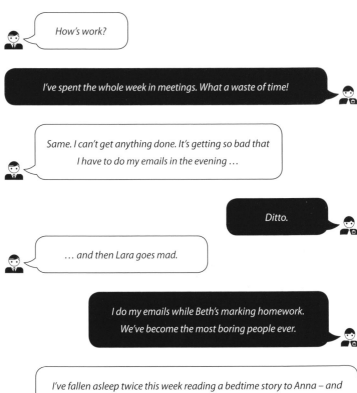

How's work?

I've spent the whole week in meetings. What a waste of time!

Same. I can't get anything done. It's getting so bad that I have to do my emails in the evening …

Ditto.

… and then Lara goes mad.

I do my emails while Beth's marking homework. We've become the most boring people ever.

I've fallen asleep twice this week reading a bedtime story to Anna – and she's gone downstairs and told Lara, 'Dad's snoring in my bed again.'

Although they have different family circumstances, Ethan and Dan are caught in patterns that don't seem to be working, but it's easier to stick with what's familiar than to make a change. When it comes to conversation, there are plenty of ways to do things differently. Here are some suggestions for ways of breaking the mould, all relatively straightforward to implement.

WHAT TO DO?

STEP 1:
Create New Routines and Make Them Habits

Try folding your arms in the way you're used to. Now fold them the other way. It'll feel wrong and uncomfortable and, chances are, you'll revert to your old routine next time. In the same way, any changes to your conversational patterns will feel awkward to start with, but persistent practice allows them to become seamlessly integrated into the section of your brain called the basal ganglia, where your habits are stored.

Here are some ideas to turn tired routines on their head. You could also try out some of your own ideas – the important thing is to find the ones that work for you and to persist with them.

At work:

- **For the first 30 minutes of your day, go and talk to people:** I recently read an article that said great leaders never start their day by wading through their emails. Whether or not this is true, it makes good sense. Emails tend to put you in reactive mode. In contrast, start your day in conversation. It creates relationship. Without this, nothing else will work.
- **Have 15-minute stand-up meetings:** These are the alternative to long meetings, where people settle in their chairs and happily give you their

opinions about life. Stand-up meetings have a different energy to them; everyone wants to keep to the point. I've seen teams meet for five minutes every hour while under pressure on a project. It creates energy and focus and shows others that you mean business.

- **Don't fill the allocated time:** If you have a team meeting that's scheduled to be an hour in length, how comes it always seems to last an hour? Why doesn't it finish early? It's because we tailor the conversation to fill the allotted time, rather than the other way around. Practise finishing meetings early and give people some time back. They'll rarely complain.

- **Have lunch together and talk:** It's becoming increasingly common for people to grab a sandwich and eat lunch in front of their computer, or to email a colleague who's sitting a few desks away. Sometimes people laugh outright when I ask them how long they allow for lunch. We'd do well to learn from our continental cousins, who don't tolerate such behaviour. They get together at lunchtimes to talk and have a complete break from their work. If you did this, the relationships you'd build would pay off over time.

- **Ask people what motivates them:** When was the last time someone asked you this question? It's perhaps the most important information for any manager, teacher or parent. Yet many people say they've never been asked it. Some people are highly motivated by achievement, success or money. For others, these have no bearing at all. They simply want to enjoy the journey and their relationships with the people around them. Try asking – and then listen.

- **Reduce attendance lists:** Always start a meeting by asking, 'Does everyone really need to be here?' Don't wind up accumulating more and more meeting attendees. Life already contains enough committees without adding any more. And, if you don't know why *you're* in a meeting, don't stay – chances are that everything will get along perfectly well without you being there.

- **Get away as a team:** If it's within your power to make this happen, go away with your work team twice a year. Use it as a chance to catch up on each other's lives, review progress, talk about personal aspirations, create your long-term strategy and discuss how you're working together. It doesn't have to be a lavish affair – I've worked with teams in a remote hostel where we've slept in dormitories for a few pounds a night. It's the experience and the time together that count.

At home:

- **Ask for an alternative birthday present:** Take advantage of your birthday to ask for people to spend time with you. A friend of mine asks each of his grown-up children for one birthday present a year, and the same one every year – to spend a weekend with him at a location of their choice, where they can drink wine, talk and be together. Try this out and turn your phone off while you're doing it. Call the place where you'll be staying and ask if they have WiFi. If they do, go somewhere else.
- **Do something away from home every week:** Conversation is easier when you aren't surrounded by all the jobs that need doing. Getting away is hard when you have young children, but you can offer to look after your friends' or families' children for an evening, or even a weekend, in exchange for them doing the same for you. When you do get away, you may need to agree a ban on spending all your time talking about the kids – or the household chores.
- **Eat where you can speak:** It's a fact that fewer than a third of US families eat dinner together regularly. Of those who do, more than half have the TV

on at the same time, which acts as an effective conversation killer. Getting away from the TV isn't easy, particularly since two-thirds of homes in the UK and the US have three TVs.[2] The challenge is made even harder with iPads and smartphones only a finger's touch away. This is an area that requires clear family ground rules. Maybe TV dinners can be the exception rather than the rule.

- **Put your phone away completely while you talk:** This principle applies equally at home and at work. Psychologists at the University of Essex conducted experiments on the impact of having a mobile phone in view while conducting a conversation.[3] Feelings of closeness and trust were reduced when a mobile phone was placed between the participants. You can test this principle for yourself by looking at your phone several times while someone's speaking to you, and then asking them what it feels like. If they're honest, they're likely to say they felt ignored or undervalued and struggled to hold your attention. Putting your phone away – completely – is the remedy.

- **Acknowledge each other more often:** Our taste buds are much more sensitized to bitter tastes than sweet ones, since bitter tastes are more likely to be toxic and need immediate rejection from the body. In the same way, negative feedback and criticism are more 'sticky' in our minds than praise or acknowledgment. As a consequence, we're liable to complain that someone 'never has a good word to say about us' or that our partner 'always finds something to criticize'. We can balance the scales by consciously finding ways to acknowledge them. This doesn't require you to pour out vacuous praise, but means being on the lookout to offer encouragement and thanks whenever they are due.

- **Consider conversation as an aphrodisiac:** I recently attended a corporate dinner during which a colleague turned to me after a couple of drinks and said, 'The greatest aphrodisiac for my wife is to go out for a coffee, shoot the breeze, and for me to listen to her.' This comment came directly after a discussion about the leadership requirements of his business, and was a bit of a surprise, but he's by no means unique. Women have been telling their partners the same for decades, yet somehow it fails to compute in a male brain in which listening is not the obvious antecedent to sex. However, men will also testify to the fact that there are few things in life that create a greater sense of connection – and experience of love – than being heard.

There's no need to shake up every part of your life, but it's worth examining any areas where your conversations have gone stale. Remember, occupying the same space as someone else is not the same as actually talking together.

The challenge is that people have different needs. The more reflective need time on their own to recharge their batteries. I met one mother who said that after a full day of interacting with clients and colleagues at work, she needed an hour on her own every day. It wasn't that she didn't love her family, but she didn't have the energy to engage with them until she'd had some private time. For her husband, the opposite was true. He got his energy from engaging with her, so they had to work out a method for both to get their needs met. This is where conversation comes into play again; enabling us to understand each other's perspective and resolve differences in expectations.

While it's true to say that changing your thinking can in turn revolutionize your behaviour, it can also work the other way round. Developing new behaviours can lead to different ways of thinking. This happens in a literal sense – new neural pathways in the brain are opened up, heralding the potential for new opportunities.

STEP 2:
Learn from Your Mistakes

A friend who teaches the violin took on a young and highly gifted student. During their first lesson she asked the student to play a piece of her own choice. Except for a brief moment when she stumbled on a note, the girl played exquisitely. My friend was impressed that she'd been able to recover her poise and continue with no further mistakes. The student, however, was appalled at her error and burst into tears. The incident demonstrated why the girl was struggling to progress – she thought she had to be note-perfect, believing that was the sole hallmark of a great musician. It was probably the consequence of previously being told that she had to 'get it right' and being scolded whenever she didn't.

Striving for mastery in any field has to involve learning from mistakes, and conversation is no exception. If we're honest, we conduct very few conversations that we could claim are close to perfect. More often than not, we're left reflecting on how we could have spoken up more assertively or listened more attentively. The marvellous thing about conversation is that it's fundamentally messy and essentially creative, and continually changes direction. The sooner we embrace this understanding, the more we can surrender to it, enjoying the process of experimenting and learning on our way to excellence.

Thomas Edison didn't ever stop believing that each negative result was taking him a step closer to a positive one. Searching every possible material that could be used as a filament for an incandescent light bulb, he tried literally thousands of alternatives before finding that carbonized cotton thread would give 15 hours of light. Even then, he wasn't content to rest on his laurels and sought tirelessly to extend the life of the filament. By the time of his death he'd registered 1,093 patents.

If we can mirror Edison's example of learning from what doesn't work, we can become ever more expert, never reaching the point where we think we have nothing more to learn. While 'doing the same thing over and over and expecting a different result' is a popular definition of insanity, trying new approaches to conversation really is the secret to improvement – as long as we learn from our mistakes.

Lesson 17: Don't fear mistakes – learn from them.

CHAPTER EIGHTEEN

REFINE YOUR STORYTELLING SKILLS
How to Use Stories to Your Advantage and Understand Other People's

Language is integral to human existence. Although many animals have remarkable methods for communicating, some of which we barely comprehend, the syntax and grammar we utilize to construct meaning are unique in their sophistication and complexity. Running alongside the development of language, and probably even supporting it, storytelling has played a starring role. Similarly, eating food together has been an important ritual for humans since prehistory, and doing that around a fire or a table lends itself to both conversation and storytelling. Before we had books, cinema, TV, mobile phones and the internet, storytelling would have been one of the most effective ways of engaging people in your ideas and points of view.

And if you stop and think about it, it's often through stories that we acquire our values – including through proverbs that go way back. When we hear someone being accused of 'crying wolf' or warn a friend that 'a leopard won't change its spots', we may have forgotten the exact detail of the original story, but its message has been passed on through conversation from one generation to the next and we understand its meaning.

DAILY STORYTELLING RITUALS

We use our storytelling skills in every dimension of life; more often than not we get to be the plucky hero in our own drama. For example:

- Late for an important meeting with a client, Ethan rehearses his get-out-of-jail story. When he gets there, his description of the traffic makes it sound as if he's been fighting an evil Time Lord. While he elaborates on the difficult traffic and roadworks he's had to struggle against, he leaves out the fact that he left home in a flap and didn't allow any margin for hold-ups. Blowing out their cheeks, the client team move on with proceedings and little harm is done. However, when Ethan followed a similar script after he got home late after his drink with Dan, Lara wasn't so amenable.

- Mia has to convince her leadership team that in the coming year she'll need more resources for her department. However, her counterparts are doing the same and there's not enough funding to go round. Each head of department puts their case forward, explaining how greater investment will bring more revenue. They need to back up their arguments with well-crunched numbers and will be held to account for their promises. Mia draws on her storytelling skills to convince her superiors that her department merits the additional funding. Any good investor, leader or manager will recognize this approach. The real test is whether or not a story is strong enough to be sufficiently believable.

- Abby's been to two parties in the last fortnight. There's another coming up and it promises to be the best of them all. She knows that Diane, her mother, will take some convincing, so she pulls on her heartstrings. She stresses that the party is the final send-off for an old childhood friend who's moving away. While it's true that her friend is leaving, the party probably won't be the last time Abby gets to say goodbye. Through her story, Abby offers Diane the chance to be a wicked witch or a fairy godmother. For her part, Diane knows she's hearing an elaboration of the truth but Abby's creative efforts help prevent an outright 'no', leading instead to a suitable compromise.

- Ravi's brother is a natural conversationalist and storyteller. He's often in demand for social occasions and, late on in proceedings, will invariably hold the floor. Someone will give him his cue – asking him to tell the story about how he met his wife or his stag night or his brief and unsuccessful stint in the army – and he'll be off. In fact, whether he's talking about his son's under-13 football match last Sunday or yesterday's team meeting at work, he makes it a work of art, pacing his pauses and intonation with skill and panache, like the conductor of an orchestra. He avoids being a bore by being self-deprecating and genuinely funny. Friends say he could make a living out of it.

Storytelling is an innate skill and part of our make-up. In their own particular way, Ethan, Mia, Abby and Ravi's brother are all storytellers. They use stories – and, when required, exaggerations – to deal with the cut and thrust of daily life. It's precisely because we do the same that, as listeners, we tolerate this – up to a point.

Being adept at storytelling doesn't mean we can't improve our skills. A few years ago, I was working with a CEO who ran a company with over 50,000 staff. He'd called together his leaders from around the globe and wanted to communicate a compelling story and vision for the company's future. After an afternoon rehearsing with him, I went off in search of a meal. When I returned later that evening to check the doors were locked and the lights were out, I found him still standing on the stage, completely alone in the huge conference room. It was 10.30pm and long after everyone else had left. Rather than thinking he was far too important and didn't need to practise, or had no room for improvement, he was still at work on his story.

GOING DEEPER WITH STORIES

While stories can help us get through the day-to-day challenges that life imposes on us, they can also have a deeper and longer-lasting impact. I can remember how, as a child, every year or two, we packed and unpacked our belongings into wooden crates as 'home' changed from Europe to Africa to Asia. When I was unable to get home from school I'd stay with my grandparents. Although eventually they acquired a television, most of our time together was spent talking and playing games.

Once in a while, I'd quiz my grandfather about his experiences during the First World War, asking tactless questions as only a child can. He was always quick to change the subject. Somehow, I'd found out that he'd been shot on the first day of the Battle of the Somme in 1916, which, by the time the sun set, had claimed 60,000 British casualties. When I asked whether he was angry to have been disabled, he exclaimed, 'Good heavens, no! I'm lucky to be alive.' I went on to ask him about the challenges of being a forester whose leading hand was a 'dud', as he described it. He told me how he'd learned to cut trees with the other one. I still have notes from him that were written in the slanted script that he'd had to develop after the war.

At the same time, I never tired of hearing my grandmother's stories about her childhood in India. Some of these were exotic tales that included close shaves with king cobras and charging elephants. Others were about her upbringing. She told me that, as a child at school in England, she didn't see her parents for eight years because the trip to India by boat was too long to merit the journey home.

My favourite was the story about how she'd met my grandfather. I'd ask her whether she'd turned down other proposals for marriage. 'Dozens!' she'd reply, with a twinkle in her eye. She explained how, once married, she and my grandfather chose to return to England with just a few belongings rather than continue the cycle of separation with their own children. As they made the six-week journey by boat, she had plenty of time to consider the limited prospects of arriving in the UK with no income, no home, a disabled husband, a baby and another one on the way. Her stories were often about faith and overcoming impossible odds, including one about the time when she was in her 30s and had repeated mastoiditis caused by middle ear infections, creating a risk of infection in her brain. After failed operations the doctors said there was no more they could do for her. She lived to be 97.

A few years ago, when I was working in South Africa for a large and prestigious organization, I had a sudden realization about the significance of my grandparents' stories. Gcina Mhlophe-Becker, one of the great African storytellers, spoke at the company's leadership conference. As I listened to her, the simple truth behind my conversations with my grandparents dawned on me. I realized that, far from boring me with their life circumstances, they'd been teaching me their values; these were the kernel held within the husk of their stories. Although the precise content of their encounters and exploits have, over time, blurred in my memory, their values have remained in sharp focus. They've had a profound influence on my life.

When my wife Sally and I faced the decision of whether or not to move our own young family abroad, my grandmother's stories seemed to ring in my ears. At the time, we too had a baby daughter, with our second daughter also due. In career terms, my prospects were promising and my employer in the US was generous and supportive, but I knew I'd be working away from home each week. In the end, we decided to stay in the UK, without knowing where I'd be working. Rather than being dismissed as tall tales from a bygone era, my grandmother's stories suddenly felt fresh and relevant.

WHAT TO DO?

STEP 1:
Refine Your Storytelling Skills

Great leaders capture people's imagination and commitment by telling vivid, compelling and believable stories – whether these describe their vision for the future or how they can serve their customers. We can all improve our skills if we pay attention to and learn from outstanding storytellers.

At tribal meetings in Mqhekezweni, where he grew up, Nelson Mandela used to listen to one speaker after another, trying to understand why one would manage to engage the audience while the words of another would fall on deaf ears. He could hardly have imagined how the skills forged in these meetings would serve him during later life – the product of his curiosity and willingness to learn.

Mike Harris claims that each of his billion-pound businesses began with his bringing together a group of people to help write the final chapter of the story. Though it was based years in the future, it gave them something to aim for. They then took the story out into the wider world, telling it to hundreds of potential customers, investors and critics. By listening to people's feedback, they were able to refine their story and to use it to focus the development of new products and services.

STEP 2:
Create Experiences That Will Lead to Shared Stories

I don't remember ever staying in a hotel until I was about 15. Summer holidays involved long car journeys and camping. We'd bicker, have endless card and ball games and climb the nearest mountain. Straggled out across the hillside, my elder brother would lead the assault while I stretched myself to stay on his heels. My mother would hold the backstop position and chivvy my sister along, while my father constantly moved between the ranks, trying to hold our ragged army together. Our holidays must have been anything but restful for my parents but, 40 years later, we still talk about them. When I became a parent, I realized that one of my most important tasks was to create shared experiences that we'll talk about for ever after.

If you camp on a slope and end up sliding into a huge bundle during the night, the chances are that you'll relive that moment for years to come in your conversations. Since we're bound together by our shared stories, make sure you create shared experiences that you'll remember and retell.

STEP 3:
Ask People about Their Stories

People's stories are fascinating, if we can be bothered to ask and listen. This isn't the same as asking for people's opinions on life; we're already on the receiving end of too many of these. When people talk about their upbringing, fears, hopes and motivations, they appear to us in a deeper and richer light.

Make time with the older generation to ask them about their stories. And we must remember that children have their own stories to tell, too. As the information age reduces the average length of our interactions, we need to make the time to share our stories with one another. Whoever invented the kitchen table must have had conversation in mind.

Lesson 18: Most conversations are quickly forgotten but great stories stay with us for life.

CHAPTER
NINETEEN

CROSS THE THRESHOLD
How to Find Your Voice and Speak Up

In his brilliant book *On Chesil Beach*, Ian McEwan tells the story of Edward and Florence falling into blame and recrimination on their wedding night. As the book opens they're making excited small talk about the future, but there's a dark subtext in the form of unvoiced concerns about sexual difficulties.

Despite her love for Edward, the prospect of a physical relationship inspires a sense of dread in Florence, but she's unable to express her fears. Edward's desire for Florence is almost overpowering, but his own unspoken fear is that he'll let himself down by producing a below-par performance on their first night. Sure enough, their encounter in bed turns into a disaster; Edward 'arrives too early', prompting Florence to flee in panic to the beach. When Edward catches up with her, their survival instincts take over. He accuses Florence of having no idea how to be with a man. Florence's response goes against the grain of her character and her true feelings for Edward when she makes a mocking comment about his sexual failure.

Aware of the damage she's done, Florence makes a last-ditch effort to repair the situation. She suggests Edward should fulfil his sexual desires with someone else. Edward can't see this for what it is – a desperate attempt to secure his love – and is outraged. When he finally arrives back at their hotel room, Florence is gone. Wedding presents are returned by post and a divorce is confirmed on the grounds of non-consummation. In an hour or two, they have got themselves into the Tangle, the Big Argument and the Bad Place. Faced with this predicament, and ill-equipped to deal with it, Florence has opted for the Lock Down.

THE COST OF WHAT WE DON'T SAY

The tragedy of Edward and Florence's story is that they don't voice their underlying fears and concerns. Much of the time it's what we *don't* say that causes the problems.

Let's take Mia and Lara's relationship as an example. They're old friends, and in their early 20s were practically inseparable. But circumstances have changed and they're both married with children now. Ravi and Ethan have little in common, so they don't tend to meet up as families. Lara has tried to contact Mia a couple of times recently about getting together on their own, but Mia's been unable to make it. She also cancelled a get-together at short notice. Lara's last text said:

```
Hi M. Hope all's well. Haven't seen you for AGES!!!
Can we catch up soon?? L xxxx
```

Mia would love to see Lara but at the moment she's struggling with life's demands. While Lara has time to meet during the day, Mia is over-stretched at work. Her team is under-resourced and they're dealing with an incredibly stressful legal case. Meanwhile, evenings and weekends are taken up with the children's homework, football, judo, dance classes and more. When she finally replies to Lara, she says:

```
Oops sorry. Things mad here. B in touch soon.
M x
```

Lara's negative bias kicks in and her thought process goes roughly like this:

> *But this is what you said last time, and you didn't call then. Your text doesn't seem like the kind of message you'd send to one of your oldest friends. It's more like something you'd send to an acquaintance. You used to be so amazingly reliable about keeping in touch; now I'm lucky to get an 'x' at the end of your text – if you reply at all. Maybe you've moved on from our friendship. Maybe Ravi doesn't want us to get together because he doesn't get on with Ethan ... maybe he's got a chip on his shoulder because Ethan's more successful than he is. It shouldn't always be down to me to contact you.*

Over the days that follow, Lara's 'maybes' become fixed views. Everything seems to be pointing her to the conclusion that Mia has moved on and isn't interested in their relationship any more. Lara even goes through her diary and discovers she's only met up with Mia once over the past nine months. During that time she's sent Mia seven texts but only had four back and one of those was to cancel their get-together.

Conclusions work in a very particular way: they take the grey out a situation so that we know how to respond. In doing so, they determine the world we see. Another way of putting this is to say we see the world *through* our conclusions, and collect evidence to support them.

In the end, Mia does get in touch and they do organize a get-together. However, Lara's unsure whether or not to raise the issue. Here are two scenarios that could unfold for her:

Scenario 1 – The thought of talking about how she feels seems awkward to Lara, so she holds back. They have a perfectly nice catch-up, but it's as though the basis of their relationship has somehow changed. Of course they're still friends, but it doesn't feel as though they're *special* friends – and this is what hurts. Lara's not sure what she's done wrong and she decides to back off from initiating contact with Mia.

Scenario 2 – Lara decides to raise the issue with Mia and thinks about how to tackle the conversation. She makes real efforts to set up the context and to express her feelings rather than her opinions. She also endeavours to be responsible for her own story and begins as follows:

> *Listen, I really hope you don't mind me raising this, but I miss not seeing you more often. We used to be in touch all the time. I know we've both got families and absurdly busy lives, so it's not going to be like the old times when we were single. I've been wondering whether you've moved on from our friendship or if there's a problem. Or have I just made all that up?*

Mia is very surprised to hear this, but the conversation doesn't escalate because Lara's done a superb job of opening it and ensuring there's no sense of accusation. What happens next is an outpouring from Mia, particularly about the stresses of work, none of which Lara was aware of. It turns out that the legal case has been a horrible ordeal. A client has been suing social services for negligence, involving members of Mia's team directly; she had to testify at the tribunal. As if that wasn't enough, they've found out that Jay has dyslexia and dyspraxia. It's not a huge problem, but it explains his disaffection with school and issues about his coordination. Their conversation enables Lara to take the second perspective on what's been happening, and completely alters her view of the past few months.

Before they leave, Mia apologizes for not including Lara in what's been going on in her life. Lara realizes that her earlier conclusions were a complete misunderstanding. She'd got into the Bad Place, but it now feels as if her issues have been completely resolved.

Crossing the threshold isn't easy, particularly when it's a difficult conversation about sex or infuriating personal habits or deep-set fears. It's important to remember that 'difficult' is a relative term. What's easy for you may be challenging for me and vice versa. Some subjects may seem too trivial to broach and you'd feel ridiculous doing so. Others can feel too hard. You may worry that raising the problem will cause deep offence and an irreparable fault-line in the relationship.

On the other hand, if you don't speak up, the problem may become so magnified in your mind that it starts to have an impact on your relationship. This can lead to your not speaking – or meeting – as often as you used to, or feeling a sense of distance when you do, or losing contact completely.

There's really no comfortable middle ground; there are consequences to speaking up and consequences to keeping quiet, and life doesn't come with a warranty that another person will be willing to talk. However, when we do cross the threshold and speak up, as Lara did, it's often less traumatic than we'd feared. A few years ago my work involved my travelling away from home a lot. I experienced a gnawing concern that my children felt I was letting them down in my role as a father. I resolved to talk to them, yet noticed I was fearful of the outcome; it was ridiculous, perhaps, but I didn't want to discover that my concerns were founded. In the end, I chose my opportunity to speak to Emily, our eldest. Our conversation went like this:

Em? You know that I've been away a lot recently.

Yes.

 Well, do you feel like I'm 'there' for you enough, as a dad?

(Without any hesitation)

Yes.

(Thinking she had misheard, I started again.)

 OK, but you know I've been travelling a lot. I feel like I'm not around enough for you …

You are, Dad, for the things that matter. I'll let you know if you're not. Can I get on with my homework now?

My other children, Rosy and Marcus, echoed Emily's sentiments. It was evident that I'd made up a huge story in my mind about how I was failing in my role. Of course, the solution was to cross the threshold and ask them. This principle is at the heart of Blamestorming – you can assume that you know what someone else is thinking or feeling, but you don't for sure until you've asked them.

WHAT TO DO?

STEP 1:
Separate Impact and Intent

Lara could have avoided getting into the Bad Place if she'd been able to distinguish between *impact* and *intent*. Here's how it works.

When something has a negative impact on us, we're inclined to think that the other person is badly motivated or has ill intentions. The more we feel hurt, let down or angry, the more we tend to blame the other person or question her motives.

In Lara's mind, it works like this:

> *I feel hurt and let down. Mia doesn't value our friendship.*

Lara's far less likely to think like this:

> *Mia has no wish or desire to cause me any hurt and yet I feel hurt and let down.*

This statement may feel like a contradiction in terms, but it's much more accurate than the first one. Separating intent and impact helps avoid getting into mental tangles.

In Edward and Florence's case it might have saved their relationship. Years on from their fateful night on the beach, and after a subsequent marriage and divorce, Edward recognizes what actually happened with Florence. He realizes that her intentions were selfless, even rather extraordinary. The impact of her proposal had been tremendous, but this didn't mean that she'd been duplicitous. If he'd been able to recognize this *in the moment*, he might have been reassuring rather than self-righteously indignant. By the time he understands what happened, Florence is long gone.

STEP 2:
Make a Choice

There isn't a law that demands that you speak up when you have an issue or problem in a relationship. Perhaps over time an immediate issue may become less significant. But, either way, it's important to make a choice in the here and now.

You can either choose not to address the difficulty and be responsible for the consequences, or choose to cross the threshold and speak up. If you decide to go with the latter, pay careful attention to giving the conversation the greatest chance for success, rather than going down the path of trying to prove that your assumptions are right.

STEP 3:
Speak Up

If you decide to speak up, there's nothing worse than beating around the bush. I don't mean that you skip the context and go straight for the jugular. Some people pride themselves on being straight-talkers who will tell you what they think whether or not you want to hear it, considering it your problem if you don't like what you're told. This works well for some people, while others will be offended, particularly when there are different cultural conventions at play. A straight-talker's intentions may be sound, but the impact can be negative.

It's important to adapt how you speak depending on who you're talking to and according to the situation. As Lara found with Mia, there are times where we need to drop the pretence and make the conversation real. Sometimes it's the conversations we don't have that mark the death-knell for our relationships.

STEP 4:
Give People Space

By the time you get round to having that difficult conversation, you may have given considerable thought to what you want to say. In contrast, it may come as a complete surprise for the person you're having it with. Be prepared for the fact that they'll need to come to terms with what they're hearing.

In her 1969 book, *On Death and Dying*, Elizabeth Kübler-Ross introduced a hypothesis based on her work with terminally ill patients. In the majority of cases she found that patients went through a spectrum of different emotional states: beginning with denial then leading to anger, bargaining, depression and acceptance. Her model has since been adapted to fit a broader set of situations where someone receives unwelcome news. The instinctive response is often to deny it, followed by feelings of anger, then withdrawal to lick their wounds and, finally, coming round to acceptance – whatever form this takes.

When making a challenging suggestion – giving difficult feedback or voicing a difficult issue – you need to give people room to voice their thoughts and feelings. If you listen to them, they're likely to reach the acceptance stage more swiftly.

Lesson 19: There is a risk to speaking up and a cost to staying silent.

CHAPTER TWENTY

UNDERSTAND YOUR IMPACT
Why Words Move Life – for Better or Worse

All kinds of expressions make a distinction between 'talk' and 'action', but most are weighted in favour of 'action'. It's true, if I talk about writing a book and never actually get round to it, then my words would be no more than hot air. But do actions always speak louder than words? I guess if we tend to be all talk and no action nothing much is going to get done, but at the same time, without talk there's a lot that wouldn't happen either. Talk can be cheap but it can also be priceless. Have you ever had a conversation that has changed your life in some way – subtle or profound?

In 1979, having nearly died following a cocaine overdose and with his life in an addiction-fuelled free-fall, jazz legend Tony Bennett was talking to Jeff Rawlins, who'd managed the comedian Lenny Bruce before Bruce died of a drugs overdose.

'I knew Lenny. What did you think of him?' Bennett asked Rawlins.

'He sinned against his talent', was the reply he got.[1]

Those five words shook Tony Bennett and pushed him onto the path of recovery. He completely turned himself around: dropped the drugs, became sober, received 16 Grammies and sold over 50 million records worldwide. As Bennett says, 'That sentence changed my life.'

Few conversations have that kind of impact, but on some level every conversation will have an effect on you. In fact, your life is constantly being influenced by conversations – and you're not even involved in a lot of them. Right now, politicians and other policymakers are having conversations that will directly affect you. Far from being cheap, their talk can end up being quite costly, with far-reaching implications for your career or the amount of taxes you pay.

On a personal level, conversations can help us make decisions, inspire us, deepen relationships and encourage us to get things done. When they go wrong, though, we can end up feeling hurt, misunderstood or betrayed.

CHICAGO TO LONDON

Some years ago, I was travelling on a night flight from Chicago to London. After a long week away in a different time zone it was a relief to get airborne. We were on schedule and I was aiming to get the 7am train home from the airport for a late breakfast with the family on Saturday morning.

We were more than halfway there when my neighbour alerted my attention to the screen on the back of the seat in front of him. On the display he was pointing at, the map of our plane's progress seemed to show that we were flying directly *away* from our destination – to Newfoundland, Canada. Other passengers had realized this too and a wave of discontent was sweeping through the plane. People stood up, intercepted flight attendants and started impromptu meetings in the aisles. Reactions ranged from annoyance to alarm and fury.

Suddenly, above all our chatter, the captain's voice broke through on the intercom. I don't know if voice-tests are part of the selection procedure for pilots, but this one had the textbook tone of a flight captain. Immediately, we were all ears.

> *Some of you will have noticed that we have changed direction. I'm sorry to say that a passenger at the front of the plane is ill and requires immediate medical assistance. We are flying to St John's in Newfoundland, where medical staff will be waiting. It will take us about two hours to get there and then we'll need to refuel before setting off again. I apologize for the disruption this*

will cause to your journey but thank you for your patience.
I'll update you in due course.

The pilot's announcement only lasted for about 20 seconds. It confirmed long delays yet, in that moment, a transformation took place in the way passengers were behaving. Despite the news of the detour, the atmosphere in the cabin suddenly changed. The general mood became one of acceptance, support and concern for a fellow passenger whose life was at stake. As we approached St John's we were diverted slightly northward to Gander, where we eventually made our landing. Even though the sick person was further up the plane, and we couldn't see anything, we sat in silence as we heard the thump of the doors opening and the sound of the paramedics rushing on board to attend to her.

When we took off again, resuming our journey to London, there were no complaints. Nor, when the plane had landed, did people start rushing for the exits. I felt a quiet pride in our dignified response and a respect for the pilot. He'd made the decision to take 200 people on a two-hour return rather than continuing to London for three to four hours. Although not long, those two hours could have given our fellow passenger the extra time that made the difference between her living or dying. It was the right call to make and we all knew it.

On the train home from the airport, I reflected on what had happened. The captain's announcement had been both brief and factual. I wondered why it had precipitated such an instantaneous change in our attitude and behaviour, and I realized that it was the meaning we'd created from his words. The captain's words formed a bond between us and in our minds we became partners in a flight to save a life. Any personal discontent dwindled into insignificance.

MEANING-MAKERS

The fact is that we humans are meaning-makers and languages of all kinds – visual and verbal – are our primary tools in the construction and reinforcement of meaning. This is both a unique advantage and a weakness. When it comes to conversation, we create significance out of what people say and what they don't say, from the way they phrase their words to the way we read their body language. A slightly raised eyebrow, a comment that tails off, a subtle change in tone or a choice of word can lead us to conclusions that may or may not be in line with the other person's intentions. It's what makes conversation so challenging, dynamic and endlessly intriguing. This can work to our advantage or against us.

In his book *Organizing Genius*, Warren Bennis outlines the characteristics of what he calls 'Great Groups' – groups of people who've collaborated in a way that allowed them to achieve remarkable accomplishments, defying historical precedents in the process. Bennis argues that the leaders of these groups create 'missions from God'. This doesn't mean that they find religion; rather, they create an extraordinary sense of collective purpose. Instead of operating within existing industries, they invent new ones. Rather than being constrained by rules, they redefine them. You won't find them saying that they spend their day 'having meetings'; they're working out how to change the world. In short, they use conversation to imbue their endeavours with meaning.

On the other hand, an unwise word, or the absence of a word, can work against us. George W. Bush must have regretted a response that he gave in 2002 on a golf course after receiving news of a suicide bombing: 'I call upon all nations to do everything they can to stop these terrorist killers. Thank you. Now watch this drive.'[2] With these words he continued his round of golf, leaving a media storm behind him.

Bush's comments may have been totally sincere, and yet his pause between 'terrorist killers' and 'Now watch this drive' – separated with a 'thank you' – was too brief. The listening world concluded that for George W. Bush, golf took precedence. The difference between compassion and dispassion can be measured in the length of a single breath.

Or take Gerald Ratner, who nearly bankrupted his company when a joke he cracked backfired. Having spent 25 years building his family jewellery business into a household name, he wiped £500 million off its share value in an instant during a speech in 1991 to 5,000 people at the Institute of Directors. In it he referred to a cut-glass sherry decanter with six glasses on a silver-plated tray that Ratners were selling for £4.95. 'People ask, "How can you sell this for such a low price?" I say, "Because it's total crap".' On top of this gaffe, Ratner went on to comment that the earrings his shops sold were, 'cheaper than a Marks & Spencer prawn sandwich but probably wouldn't last as long.' Just a few words cost Ratner his £650,000 salary and slashed his billion-pound turnover in seconds. His speech features in Stephen Weir's book, *History's Worst Decisions* – along with Eve eating the apple and Nero destroying Rome.[3]

The greatest leaders understand the profound impact conversation can have and seek to master its skills. The best sports coaches are no different, learning when to acknowledge someone's efforts and when to challenge them. Wonderful teachers take the same approach. Test this by casting your mind back to your school days. Which teachers killed your interest in a subject? They might have been technically proficient, but it's likely that they were pretty dry and monotonous. They may not have lacked the power of speech, but they probably lacked proficiency in the art of conversation and any skill in speaking and listening. We've all had teachers like this, but also one or two who held our interest and sparked our curiosity.

With these inspiring people, we were motivated to learn and develop – we probably owe them a debt of gratitude for our subsequent life decisions and relative success.

WHAT TO DO?

STEP 1:
Ask How You're Doing

Find out what impact your conversations are having on other people. There have been instances in my work when I've asked a manager how an important conversation with one of the staff has gone. 'Yeah, it was great,' came the reply. But the report from the team member didn't concur at all. They felt lectured and spoken down to – ending up in the Bad Place. The best way of finding out how effective your conversations are is by asking. It's a relatively simple thing to do but we'd often rather not ask in case we find out something we don't want to hear.

Benjamin Zander is one of the world's leading conductors. He gives the members of his orchestra a white sheet of paper in every rehearsal so they can offer comments, ideas or feedback. Start adopting the same principle. Following a work conversation you have with a peer, perhaps during the next day, ask if they have any thoughts or insights they didn't mention the day before. Then listen. If they take the opportunity you've offered and give you feedback, you'll invariably learn something useful. And if you take action based on what they say, they're more likely to offer unprompted feedback next time. It's a way of developing relationships based on a sense of trust and partnership.

STEP 2:
Ask What Will Make a Difference

Take the position of a sports coach at half time during a game. In this situation, there's little value in defending your opinions or trying to convince others that you're in the right. The only question that's relevant is, 'What will make the biggest difference to the second half?' This requires stepping outside the situation for a moment. In the same way, when you're midway through an important conversation, ask yourself what will make the biggest impact on its second half. You'll get a totally different outcome from the one you'll get if you fall back on your opinions and merely try to push *your* point of view.

Whether you're supporting your children through their exams, having a challenging discussion with someone at work or delivering a critical project, it's worth asking what conversation would have the greatest impact on what happens next, either for an individual or team. You don't always have to have a solution – sometimes the best thing to do is simply to listen.

Lesson 20: Conversation can move life – that's why we invented it.

**CHAPTER
TWENTY
ONE**

TAKE ON A LIFETIME OF PRACTICE
Why Practice Is More Important Than Perfection

We might start a conversation with a clear intention, yet it can still fail to go to plan. There's a greeting card showing Tarzan preparing to traverse the treetops to announce his love to Jane. He practises his speech and then swings over to her on a leafy rope. To his horror, when he opens his mouth, all that comes out is: 'Me Tarzan, you Jane'.

The English conductor Sir Thomas Beecham told the story of how he was walking down the street one day when he met a woman he recognized. Unfortunately, for the life of him he couldn't remember who she was and pretended to know her while asking questions that, he hoped, would reveal her identity. He asked after her health, and she said she was well. He enquired after her family, and was told they were fine. Getting a little desperate, he remembered she had a brother. He asked what he was up to. 'He's still King,' replied Princess Victoria.[1]

We all have times when, for one reason or another, we muck up a conversation. We get people confused with each other, make unfortunate comments, email the wrong person or fall victim to the aberrations of predictive text. I once wrote a message to a senior executive in which I referred to 'the thing' I'd sent him; he was a bit surprised to see me asking about 'the thong'. Such a mistake is now commonly referred to as GSMU (Ground Swallow Me Up).

CONTINUAL IMPROVISATION

When you consider the complexities involved in having a conversation, it's actually surprising that we don't make more mistakes. Since we don't have direct access to other people's thoughts, we have to rely on the difficult art of language – and meaning construction – to convey our pictures of the world to each other. This process is both remarkable and highly imprecise. People don't say exactly what they mean, so we're constantly trying to fill in the gaps in our understanding in order to create a coherent picture from the pieces we're given.

To help the process, we evaluate a multitude of non-verbal cues while trying to hear what they're *actually* saying and simultaneously pulling together our own thoughts in preparation for a response. Once we become the speaker, we use our personal lexicon to convey our views and opinions before another switch occurs. It all happens at lightning speed – like a downhill skier adapting, in each moment, to the conditions under his feet. For most of the time we take this process for granted, and it's a testament to the miracle of the human brain that it usually works so seamlessly. However, it consumes vast reserves of energy – which explains why you can spend a day in meetings and feel physically wrecked at the end of it.

People admire actors who're able to improvise on the spot, often saying they couldn't possibly do it themselves. In reality we're all in the business of improvising. Conversation demands it because we don't know for sure how other people will react. We have questions that can't be answered in advance. If I speak my true feelings, will I get rejected? If I challenge my manager, will my career be cut short? If I raise that issue with my friend, will she take offence? We make internal predictions about the likely outcome and our negative bias is inclined to convince us it's safer to avoid speaking up. The long-term costs include love not getting expressed, issues not being addressed and damaging conclusions being drawn that create rifts in our friendships.

There are no guarantees that a conversation will turn out for the better if you speak up. However, it is possible to increase the odds that the outcome will be successful.

DESTROY THE MYTHS

To start developing your skills in conversation you'll need to dismantle some popular myths:

Myth 1: *You're either good at conversation or you're not* – some people are naturally more social and extroverted than others. They may speak confidently but, bearing in mind that conversation requires both speaking and listening, this doesn't mean they're better at it. Whatever your character, you can always improve. And, unlike the double bass player or pianist, who would struggle if they wanted to take their instruments everywhere with them, conversation can be practised wherever there's a person to speak to.

Myth 2: *Conversational skills can't be taught* – it's true that conversational skills tend to be developed through trial and error, in the hustle and bustle of daily life. But it's also true that you can take them to another level if you're willing to develop new techniques and engage in mindful practice. Let's take our memory as an analogy. Many people say that theirs is like a sieve, yet the world's greatest memory champions claim that their innate memory is no better than anyone else's. Three-times world champion Ben Pridmore, who once memorized 27 packs of cards in an hour, insists that he never amazed his friends in the playground at school with his powers of recall.[2] He simply decided, as an adult, to practise tried-and-tested techniques that allowed him to tap into the brain's unused potential for filing and recalling information. 'Anybody can do it,' he says. Similarly, when it comes to conversation, the same benefits are available to all of us; if we can be bothered to invest our time and effort in ongoing practice.

Myth 3: *Talk is cheap* – saying that talk is cheap is no different to saying that wine is cheap; it can be, but it can also be wildly expensive. Some conversations will have little impact on the direction of our lives while others will have a lasting effect – for better or worse. We've all experienced the benefit of conversations that have gone right, as well as the cost of conversations that have gone wrong; from friendships to relationships or job interviews.

Myth 4: *I'm too old to change* –the idea that you're too old to improve is nonsense. As long as we're able to speak and listen, we have the capacity to improve. In a passport control queue at a Spanish airport, I once overheard people in front of me laughing with the official – a rare occurrence. As I stepped forward, I saw two officials, side by side, in the smallest of security cabins. In age, they were probably approaching 60. One of them looked at our passports and then, in broken English, explained what they were doing: 'We try to better make our English,' he said. 'Can we practise?' Rather taken aback by this unfamiliar routine, I nodded and waited to see what would happen next. Drawing his shoulders up, he announced in his best possible accent, complete with arm movements: 'The formula for shopping is that way! And the formula for the plane is that way!' It made my day, and reminded me that it's never too late to learn.

WHAT HAPPENS NEXT?

Once you've debunked the myths, it's all about practice. Over time, this is what happens:

- Daniel and Beth learn to develop their skills. Like high divers who can prevent injury by pulling out midway through a routine that's gone wrong, they find that it's possible to press the stop button during arguments that are becoming toxic. With the benefit of a little space and reflection, they adopt the second and third perspective and drop the Dominatricks. They're more conscious about the impact of comparisons and threats and use them with their eyes open.

- Diane finds that she gets a better reaction from Abby and Ben when she expresses her feelings rather than her opinions. Sometimes she forgets and flies off the handle, prompting the Big Argument, but these occasions are becoming fewer. She finds that if they create clear agreements, the process of resolving an argument becomes easier and that she and Abby are less often on tenterhooks with each other.

- Ethan and Dan realize that Lily is quite lonely and often just wants to be listened to. When they listen to their mother instead of trying to fix her problems, she has no need to go into Yes, But … and they don't get into the Tangle. On the other hand, when Dan is speaking to Bill, who's addicted to fixing, he understands that Bill's intentions are harmless, even though his words can be insensitive.

- When Lara and Mia manage to resolve their differences, their friendship becomes stronger than ever. In fact, it feels unbreakable because they are confident that they'll be able to engage in difficult conversations whenever they need to.

There is no Hollywood fix for any of these characters. Life doesn't work like that, and conversation is too messy to provide a perfect ending. On occasions they're all still prone to shotgun responses, which lead to the Bad Place, the Tangle and even the Lock Down. However, when this happens, they're equipped to repair the situation through their subsequent conversations. Increasingly, they find that they can have mindful conversations in which they notice and respond to the warning lights as they appear.

WHAT TO DO?

STEP 1:
Stay Humble

I've already referred to my meeting with Tim Gallwey a number of years ago. To me, he represented the epitome of an effective coach. During a group session with him he asked us what score, out of 10, we'd give ourselves as a coach of others. I considered the depth of my experience and weighed up whether I should give myself an 8 or an 8.5. As we went around the room, most people offered scores in this region – after all, we considered ourselves to be quite accomplished in our field. Someone had the presence of mind to ask Tim how he'd score himself. He gave himself a rating of 6.5. At this point we suddenly felt as though we'd massively over-shot in terms of our own self-evaluation.

That day was a lesson for me and it's been borne out in my experience; the more I learn, the more I still have to learn. Rather than being an endless source of disappointment and frustration, this realization is hugely liberating. I can stop trying to be perfect or a know-it-all or indispensable. I hope that I can contribute, to the best of my abilities, while still stretching to improve further. As George Bernard Shaw said, 'The single biggest problem in communication is the illusion that it has taken place.' If I keep this in mind, it helps me to stay humble.

STEP 2:
Keep Practising

As a student, I loved the story of Henri Matisse. He became one of the finest artists of the 20th century, despite displaying little ability or interest in art during his youth. In fact, while he was studying for his law exams in Paris, he didn't even visit the Louvre. It wasn't until he was recovering from appendicitis at the age of 21, when he was given a box of paints to help him convalesce, that he ended up painting, and continued to do so every day for the next 60 years.

While Matisse would admit that aptitude has a role to play in being a great artist, his story is a victory for application over born genius. In the months before his death in his mid-80s, he was still stressing the importance of both maintaining a curious mind and being dedicated to practice. Reading his letters and interviews, it is clear that his sense of freedom became more intense as he became more curious. He made no apology for being a lifelong student at heart. Despite the fact that his work hung in galleries all over the world, he found the idea that he'd mastered his medium laughable.

The same could be said in relation to conversation. After 30 or 40 more years of practice, I hope to become really good at it.

Lesson 21: When it comes to conversation, there is no destination.

NOTES

Chapter 1

[1] The *Oxford English Dictionary* says that conversation involves talk, and it defines the verb 'talk' as 'speak in order to give information or express ideas or feelings; converse or communicate by spoken words.' For *Blamestorming*, I am creating a wider definition of conversation, to reflect the fact that we are increasingly communicating in new ways. In doing so, I am moving closer to the original Latin word *conversari*, which meant to 'keep company'. The current meaning of the verb 'to converse' only emerged in the early 17th century.

Chapter 2

[1] The shotgun response is referred to by Daniel Kahneman as the 'mental shotgun' in his outstanding book, *Thinking Fast and Slow*, Farrar, Straus and Giroux, New York, 2011. He is describing the brain's continual assessment of threat levels and our generation of immediate answers in which speed of response and energy conservation take precedence over accuracy or mindful thinking.
[2] See article on Ellen Langer by Cara Feinberg, 'The Mindfulness Chronicles', *Harvard Magazine*, September–October 2010, pp. 41–47, 71, http://harvardmag.com/pdf/2010/09-pdfs/0910-42.pdf

Chapter 3

[1] 'Samuel Goldwyn, Biography', IMDb, http://www.imdb.com/name/nm0326418/bio

Chapter 4

[1] Taken from 'How to Get Along for 500 Days Alone Together', *BBC Online News Magazine*, 1 March 2013, http://www.bbc.co.uk/news/magazine-21619765

Chapter 5

[1] The Air Florida Flight 90 report can be found in the National Transportation Safety Board, 'Aircraft Accident Report', 13 January 1982, http://libraryonline.erau.edu/online-full-text/ntsb/aircraft-accident-reports/AAR82-08.pdf
[2] Ten Colossus machines were in use by the end of the Second World War, decoding encrypted messages between German High Command and German army commands across Europe. See http://www.bletchleypark.org.uk/content/hist/worldwartwo/stratciphers.rhtm

Chapter 6

[1] For Huey Long's filibusters, see http://www.senate.gov/artandhistory/history/minute/Huey_Long_Filibusters.htm

[2] See the Prince's Trust Youth Index 2013, based on 2,136 interviews with 16–25-year-olds, at http://www.princes-trust.org.uk/about_the_trust/what_we_do/research/youth_index_2013.aspx

Chapter 8

[1] From 'Letters to His Son by the Earl of Chesterfield, On the Fine Art of Becoming a Man of the World and a Gentleman', http://www.gutenberg.org/files/3361/3361-h/3361-h.htm

Chapter 9

[1] This illusion is named after its discoverer Hermann Ebbinghaus (1850–1909) and was popularized in a textbook by Edward B. Titchener in 1901.

[2] Amy Sutherland, 'I Trained My Husband Like an Exotic Animal', *The Week*, 7 October 2006. The article first appeared in the *New York Times*.

Chapter 10

[1] For a full transcript of Geoffrey Howe's speech, see http://www.emersonkent.com/speeches/resignation_speech_howe.htm

[2] For a definition of unparliamentary language in the UK parliament, see http://www.parliament.uk/site-information/glossary/unparliamentary-language/

[3] From the indexes of the *New Zealand Parliamentary Debates*, http://www.parliament.nz/en-nz/about-parliament/history-buildings/history/special/language/00PlibHstBldgsHistorySpecialLanguage1/unparliamentary-language

[4] Official statistics for casualties during the construction work for the Olympic Games state the following: 1996 Barcelona = 2 deaths; 2000 Sydney = 1; 2004 Greece = 14; 2008 Beijing = 10; 2012 London = 0. See 'London Olympics Construction is Safest in Recent Times', *Engineering News Record*, 30 July 2012, http://enr.construction.com/business_management/safety_health/2012/0730-london-olympics-construction-is-safest-in-recent-times.asp

[5] See 'To Have and to Hold ... for 87 Years!', Mail Online, 1 November 2012, http://www.dailymail.co.uk/femail/article-2226145/Worlds-longest-married-couple-Husband-wife-100-spent-87-happy-years-together.html

Chapter 11

[1] See Corporate Leadership Council, 'Driving Performance and Retention through Employee Engagement', 2004, http://www.mckpeople.com.au/SiteMedia/w3svc161/Uploads/Documents/760af459-93b3-43c7-b52a-2a74e984c1a0.pdf

[2] See Gallup Consulting's report by James

H. Harter et al, 'Q12 Meta-Analysis', 2006, http://strengths.gallup.com/private/Resources/Q12Meta-Analysis_Flyer_GEN_08%2008_BP.pdf

Chapter 12

[1] According to a survey of 1,100 people conducted by Esure, quoted in Brendan O'Neill, 'Sorry to Say', *BBC Online News Magazine*, 8 January 2007, http://news.bbc.co.uk/1/hi/magazine/6241411.stm
[2] From Plato, *Apology*, trans Benjamin Jowett, http://classics.mit.edu/Plato/apology.html
[3] Shakespeare, *Macbeth*, Act 2, Scene 2.

Chapter 13

[1] An edited extract from *Quirkology* by Dr Richard Wiseman was reproduced as 'The Truth about Lying', *Guardian*, 21 April 2007, http://www.theguardian.com/science/2007/apr/21/weekendmagazine
[2] From Dr Alan Porter's letter to *The Times*, reprinted in *The Week*, 7 January 2012.

Chapter 14

[1] Story told by Zen Buddhist monk and scholar Hara Tanzan (1819–92).
[2] From an interview with Jobs in *Business Week* in 2004, reprinted in 'Steve Jobs: In his own Words, *Telegraph*, 6 October 2011, http://www.telegraph.co.uk/technology/steve-jobs/8811892/Steve-Jobs-in-his-own-words.html

[3] For the full text of Mandela's Cape Town speech see: http://www.anc.org.za/show.php?id=4520
[4] See John Carlin, 'Mandela's Rock (Part Two)', *Guardian*, 8 June 2008, http://www.theguardian.com/lifeandstyle/2008/jun/08/women.features1

Chapter 15

[1] See 'Grigory Romanov, Former Member of U.S.S.R.'s Politburo, Dies at 85', *New York Times*, 3 June 2008, http://www.nytimes.com/2008/06/03/world/europe/03iht-obits.4.13433418.html?_r=0
[2] The story is recounted as 'Roddy Doyle Ha Ha Ha?', at http://www.anecdotage.com/articles/502/
[3] See Cognisco, '$37 Billion – US and UK Businesses Count the Cost of Employee Misunderstanding', press release, 18 June 2008, http://www.marketwire.com/press-release/37-billion-us-and-uk-businesses-count-the-cost-of-employee-misunderstanding-870000.htm
[4] From the Marine Accidents Investigation Board report submitted 5 June 1990 by Captain P.B. Marriott, http://www.maib.gov.uk/cms_resources.cfm?file=/dft_masafety_031165.pdf
[5] From the Marine Accidents Investigation Board report submitted 29 July 1987 by Wreck Commissioner, Hon. Mr Justice Sheen, http://www.maib.gov.uk/cms_resources.cfm?file=/Part_1.pdf

[6] See Mark Steyn, 'The Man Who Gave Us Newt', *National Review*, 22 January 2012, http://www.nationalreview.com/corner/288873/man-who-gave-us-newt-mark-steyn

Chapter 16

[1] See Steve Bradt, 'Wandering Mind Not a Happy Mind', *Harvard Gazette*, 11 November 2010, http://news.harvard.edu/gazette/story/2010/11/wandering-mind-not-a-happy-mind/

[2] See R.D. Rogers and S. Monsell, 'Depth of Processing and the Retention of Words in Episodic Memory', *Journal of Experimental Psychology: General*, 124(2), 1995, pp. 207–31, Table 2 of Experiment Cluster #1.

[3] 2013 report from the American Academy of Pediatrics: http://www.tes.co.uk/article.aspx?storyCode=6370742#.Uzl_FKU7UfM

Chapter 17

[1] David Rock and Jeffrey Schwartz, 'The Neuroscience of Leadership', *Strategy + Business*, 43, 2006, http://www.oncourse.com.au/articles/Neuroscience%20and%20leadership.pdf

[2] Laura Roberts, 'Two Thirds of British Households Have Three Televisions', *Telegraph*, 8 October 2010, http://www.telegraph.co.uk/finance/newsbysector/retailandconsumer/8049892/Two-thirds-of-British-households-have-three-televisions.html

[3] A.K. Przybylski and N. Weinstein, 'Can you Connect with Me Now? How the Presence of Mobile Communication Technology Influences Face-to-Face Conversation Quality', *Journal of Social and Personal Relationships*, 30(3), 2013, pp. 237–46, first published online 19 July 2012, http://intl-spr.sagepub.com/content/30/3/237.full.pdf+html

Chapter 20

[1] From Howard Reich, 'Tony Bennett Coming to Ravinia, Signs Deal with Stevie Wonder', *Chicago Tribune*, 25 August 2009, http://articles.chicagotribune.com/2009-08-25/entertainment/0908240253_1_tony-bennett-collaboration-jazz-genius

[2] This comment was made famous by Michael Moore's 2004 documentary, *Fahrenheit 9/11*.

[3] Stephen Weir, *History's Worst Decisions*, New Holland, London, 2009.

Chapter 21

[1] This possibly apocryphal story is recounted in 'Thomas Beecham', http://en.wikipedia.org/wiki/Thomas_Beecham

[2] See Stephen Robb, 'How a Memory Champ's Brain Works', *BBC Online News Magazine*, 7 April 2009, http://news.bbc.co.uk/1/hi/magazine/7982327.stm

FURTHER READING

Bennis, W. and Biederman, P.W., *Organizing Genius*, Nicholas Brealey, London, 1997

Bohm, D., *On Dialogue*, Routledge, London, 1996

Carlin, J., *Playing the Enemy: Nelson Mandela and the Game that Made the Nation*, Penguin, New York, 2008

Flam, J., *Matisse on Art*, Phaidon, Oxford, 1973

Gallwey, W.T., *The Inner Game of Tennis*, Jonathan Cape, London, 1975

Gottman, J. and Silver, N., *The Seven Principles for Making Marriage Work*, Weidenfeld & Nicolson, London, 1999

Harris, M., *Find your Lightbulb*, Capstone Publishing, Chichester, 2008

Kahneman, D., *Thinking Fast and Slow*, Farrar, Straus and Giroux, New York, 2011

Lee, N. and Lee, S., *The Marriage Book*, Alpha International, London, 2000

Mandela, N., *The Long Walk to Freedom*, Little, Brown, London, 1994

Peters, S., *The Chimp Paradox*, Vermilion, London, 2011

ACKNOWLEDGMENTS

I am proud to have brilliant partners who have contributed to *Blamestorming*. Robert Kirby at United Agents believed in me when others didn't, bringing his unique vision and tireless support. Owen Smith helped me to find my literary voice and refine every word. His generous and thoughtful spirit pervades each page. Sandra Rigby, Fiona Robertson, Suzanne Tuhrim and the rest of the team at Watkins have provided unwavering encouragement and expert guidance.

Numerous friends and family have provided tireless support. Christa Munns and Soo Spector read my early rambles and reassured me that I was on the right lines. Rob Archer and Marcus Paine gave feedback and support over months that stretched into years, without showing outward signs of exasperation.

Blamestorming has occupied countless hours that would otherwise have been family time. It is only the most generous of souls who would retain a sense of humour while urging me to continue on such an uncertain journey. My wife Sally and our children, Emily, Rosy and Marcus, have given me the room to fly. It is my greatest aspiration to do the same for them.